A Delicious 12-Week Nutrition Plan to Improve Your Child's Academic and Athletic Performance

EATING FOR A's

Alexander Schauss, Barbara Friedlander Meyer, and Arnold Meyer

POCKET
BOOKS
NONFICTION
72814·8
$9.00 U.S.
$12.00 CAN.

ISBN 0-671-72814-8

9 780671 728144

50900

Other Books by Alexander Schauss

Nutrition and Behavior
Zinc and Eating Disorders
Nutrition and Criminal Behavior: The Theories
  (Japanese publication)

Other Books by Barbara Friedlander Meyer

Earth Water Fire Air
The Great Garlic Cookbook
Cooking for a Crowd Naturally

EATING FOR A's

A Delicious 12-Week Nutrition Plan to Improve Your Child's Academic and Athletic Performance

—

Alexander Schauss,
Barbara Friedlander Meyer,
AND
Arnold Meyer

POCKET BOOKS
New York   London   Toronto   Sydney   Tokyo   Singapore

An *Original* Publication of Pocket Books

POCKET BOOKS, a division of Simon & Schuster Inc.
1230 Avenue of the Americas, New York, NY 10020

Schauss, Alexander G.
    Eating for A's : a delicious 12-week nutrition plan to improve
your child's academic and athletic performance / Alexander Schauss,
Barbara Friedlander Meyer, and Arnold Meyer.
        p.   cm.
    Includes bibliographical references and index.
    ISBN 0-671-72814-8 : $9.00
    1. Children—Nutrition.   2. Children—Health and hygiene.
3. Cookery (Natural foods)   I. Meyer, Barbara Friedlander, 1934– .
    II. Meyer, Arnold, 1942– .   III. Title.
RJ206.S37   1991
649'.3—dc20   91-16014
                                                              CIP

First Pocket Books trade paperback printing September 1991

10   9   8   7   6   5   4   3   2

I would like to dedicate this book to my children, Evan and Nova; my wife, Laura; and the late Govind Atmaram Dhopeshwarkar, adjunct professor in the School of Public Health at the University of California, and author of *Nutrition and Brain Development*, whose sudden death at an early age denied all of us much additional knowledge on the role of nutrition on brain function.

—ALEXANDER SCHAUSS

FOR GODCHILDREN:
Nuri,
Sarah, Naomi, and Reuven—
May the spark of desire to learn
and keep learning
forever be kindled in your eyes.

AND FOR JESSIE BANKOFF LEIBOWITZ
Forty years of loving devotion
to nourishing the minds
of young children.

—ARNOLD AND BARBARA MEYER

ACKNOWLEDGMENTS

*Our deepest gratitude to our editors,
Leslie Wells and Molly Allen. We also
thank our outstanding literary agent,
Heide Lange.*

PREFACE

Evidence continues to accumulate that nutrition can alter behavior. Eating correctly can help to maximize intellectual potential. The information contained in *Eating for A's* will provide the reader with the information necessary to provide optimal nutritional guidance to children. Your child may not garner a coveted scholarship as a consequence of applying the nutritional principles described in this book, but you, as a parent, will have the satisfaction of knowing that your child's eating habits did not hamper his or her scholastic achievement. Even if children don't graduate *summa cum laude* after reading this book and adopting its nutritional policies, they can look forward to a lifetime of better health.

FRANK A. OSKI, M.D.
Given Professor and Chairman
Department of Pediatrics
Johns Hopkins University
School of Medicine

CONTENTS

— *Introduction* —

Is your child more intelligent than his grades? Does your child have unrealized athletic potential? Is your child's behavior undermining his abilities?

If you answered yes to any of these questions, then *Eating For A's* is for your family. It's the first meal program specifically aimed at raising a child's academic and athletic performance. It accomplishes this by enriching the brain with 12 specific "learning nutrients" on a daily basis. These "learning nutrients" are the heart of the Eating For A's Program, and will improve a child's ability to think, remember, and solve problems.

Many children spend years on the borderline of academic achievement. As the latest statistics prove, their efforts are constantly undermined by poor diets. Up until now, no one has isolated the 12 nutrients vital to learning and created a delicious meal program around them. By identifying the foods in which they are found, and placing them in recipes, the Eating For A's Program specifically aims at improving your child's:

- long-term memory
- physical fitness
- sustained concentration
- language skills
- computational ability
- abstract thinking

1

It accomplishes this through a step-by-step three-month practical program, which stresses gradual diet change as a way of improving a child's overall achievement.

Eating For A's is not just about getting higher marks, however. Good marks are important, but not every child can be an A student. What every child *can* be, however, is nurtured in a way that allows him to get an A for *best effort*. The handicapped children who capture our attention in the Special Olympics are awarded gold medals for winning races. We don't watch them to admire their grace and fluidity of movement. They can't run as well or think as fast as non-handicapped, more intelligent children. But what they show us through their shining spirit is the excellence of their best effort. And isn't that what we want for our own children: that they try their hardest, do their best—and feel good about themselves in the process?

Often, however, to please them and see them happy, we *stress their systems with rich foods,* or foods containing too much sugar and salt. Instead, we could feed them in ways that nourish the higher learning centers of their minds and strengthen their bodies. By teaching children how to eat healthfully in their formative years, the *Eating For A's* Program instills food preferences that affect children's well-being over a lifetime.

If you're the parent of children aged 5 to 13, *Eating For A's* may not only change their lives—it could easily prolong them. The three leading causes of death in America are heart disease, cancer, and stroke—and the food one eats is directly linked to all of them. That's why the Eating For A's Program stresses the importance of changing children's outlook regarding food. Unlike other diet programs, the authors don't ask parents to keep a daily mental tabulation, wondering "Did my child get enough vitamins and minerals? Were there too many sweets? Is there enough protein and fiber?" Instead, we have created a program that is compatible with today's life-style. It tells what the best sources of the learning nutrients are, and shows how to best present them in the daily diet.

The program is the result of a combination of 45 years of nutrition studies and 34 years of research background and observation on the part of the authors. Alexander Schauss, the director of the Life Sciences Division of the American Institute for Biosocial Research, is a leading authority on the effects of nutrition and behavior. He was recently named the co-discoverer of a new treatment technique for the sometimes fatal eating disorder anorexia nervosa, and he has been involved in a series of pioneering studies examining the role of diet on deviant behavior and learning impairments. Active in sports throughout his life, Schauss is a former indoor/ outdoor track and field athlete, and has also coached an award-winning women's track and field team.

Barbara Friedlander Meyer was the nutrition education and training supervisor for the New York City school system for eight years. She inaugurated and administered a vast program of innovative nutrition education projects. She helped to revamp the breakfast and lunch programs by introducing a range of more healthful, nutritious foods. In an independent university study, this food program, administered to 600,000 New York City schoolchildren, was cited as a factor in producing one of the largest recorded gains in academic test scores in American educational history.

Arnold Meyer was the director of media for the Office of School Food and Nutrition Services for New York City's Board of Education, and the editor-in-chief of its nutrition education newspaper, *Feedback*.

1

THE ROAD TO PEAK PERFORMANCE

- Good behavior
- Scholastic excellence
- Physical fitness

In today's competitive world, these three qualities might seem to assure a child's future success. Certainly they are qualities we'd like to see in our own children—especially when they're slumped on the couch, watching television and munching potato chips.

"Are you sure you've done all your homework?" we ask. They turn to us wide-eyed, surprised at the question. With absolute conviction they reply, "Yes." But when they bring home their report cards and we stare at their mediocre marks, we know they're underperforming.

Why are they? Let's analyze the qualities on which they are marked.

Good behavior, of course, is more than just the ability to exhibit good manners. It shows that a child has learned to control his impulses and not be controlled *by* them.

5

Scholastic excellence means more than just doing homework and studying for tests. It is also a measure of a child's ability to remain mentally alert for hours on end.

Physical fitness is not simply a talent for playing sports. It also indicates a properly developed cardiovascular system, good hand-eye coordination, and quick reflexes.

The fact that food can enhance these qualities is seldom taken into consideration. No matter what we think about the well-rounded child, we never imagine him sitting down and eating. Yet a child's behavior is influenced by the chemical reactions of his food choices. His brain is constantly utilizing specific nutrients to think clearly. His physical fitness depends upon a keen respect for his health. And when children change the way they eat, everything changes.

Ricky: A Case History

Ricky is a good example to illustrate this point. A 9-year-old, he lived with two brothers, a sister, and his mom in a suburb of Seattle, Washington. His mother, a college graduate, had hopes that Ricky would also attend college. However, his prospects were poor and getting worse. His schoolwork averaged a C−. His teachers reported that he wasn't attentive to classwork and that his behavior was sometimes disruptive. And recently he had quit the track team because, in his own words, "I'd rather just come home and watch TV."

Within three months of beginning the Eating for A's Program, his grades rose to A's and B's. He rejoined the track team and impressed the coach with his new dedication to running; the teachers described his behavior as "significantly improved," and remarked that he was "much more attentive in class."

What happened?

Ricky's eventual success began when his mother Phyllis attended a nutrition lecture at her church given by a local physician. He stressed that parents had to become informed about their children's diet and its effects on their health. "Our children are educated about nutrition in ways that are disastrous," he said. "They get their information from the 13,000 food and soft drink commercials they watch over the course of a year." He went on to describe the importance of giving children specific nutrients to feed their brains.

That led Phyllis to bring Ricky to the American Institute of Biosocial Research (AIBR), where Alexander Schauss had been involved in researching brain nutrients for several years.

"What's your son's diet like?" was the first question he asked her.

"Like other boys his age," she said.

"If that's the case," he replied, "then we have a lot of work to do."

His suggestions to her became the basis of the Eating For A's Program.

First, he asked Phyllis to assess Ricky's overall physical fitness, appearance, and behavior after eating certain meals.

Then he asked her to monitor what Ricky was eating.

Third, he introduced a gradual diet change that increased the levels of specific vitamins and minerals, or "learning nutrients," used by the brain. At the same time he decreased foods that were excessively high in fat, salt, sugar, and food additives.

Fourth, he stressed the importance of using specific kinds of family interaction to encourage Ricky's cooperation in the program.

And fifth, and perhaps most important, he stressed that the changes she hoped for would probably take about three months because the effect of the program was cumulative.

Why Eating For A's Is a Three-Month Program

The Eating For A's Program is based on a 12-week cycle for two reasons. First, children's eating habits can only be changed gradually. The program begins with a sampling of tasty new foods that are added to their plates in small quantities. Bit by bit, these new foods are increased so that a child doesn't feel suddenly deprived of the foods that he's been used to. Eventually, children come to understand that nothing is being taken away from them, but rather that delicious substitutes are being offered.

For example, you'll learn a recipe for vegetable-turkey hamburgers for children who hate "carrots and all things green." After a patty or two, we've seen kids complain they couldn't get enough of them (filled with those horrible carrots and green things). And ten months later we've seen the same children contentedly munching on carrot sticks. There is some research showing evidence that exposing children to greater varieties of food increases their range of food choices later in life.

Second, because children are constantly growing and have high energy demands, they need to take in plenty of calories. This is especially true in the afternoon, when they get most of these calories from eating and drinking snacks high in sugar, fat, and cholesterol. But these snacks are not just a taste preference. Children's hormonal systems become dependent on them to get a "boost" for lagging energy. And three months is the time it takes for a child's hormonal system to adjust to the elimination of these unhealthy snacks. During this 12-week changeover period, children will stop craving sweets, or a "sugar rush," to feel good. In fact, they eventually learn that a "sugar rush" is less enjoyable than experiencing a sustained level of energy all the time.

We've been surprised at how many children not only have given up junk foods but have become disinterested in eating them when offered by their friends. Children aren't dumb, they just need to experience pleasurable alternatives.

Maximizing a Child's Potential

The Eating For A's Program offers a systematic method of maximizing a child's potential by looking at the *whole* child. There's a synergy between his academic and physical performance and his behavior—they're all interconnected. As a child feels more fit, he tackles more schoolwork. As schoolwork becomes easier to complete, he increasingly takes on more challenges. Inevitably, this results in an increased sense of confidence. As his success becomes more evident to his parents, teachers, and friends, his self-esteem increases, which encourages him to do even more.

To accomplish this he'll have to make one major sacrifice: the gradual relinquishing of junk foods and unhealthy snacks, the consumption of which is constantly encouraged on TV.

Not only has television forever changed *the way* we feed our children, it has actually *created children's eating habits*. Youngsters are especially vulnerable to TV because they can't tell the difference between what's good for them, and what's a good commercial. And a recent survey indicated that 78 percent of all kids influence what their parents buy at the grocery store.

It's been estimated that by the time your child is 18 years old, he* will have watched close to 20,000 food commercials—80 percent of which are for junk foods. Children's food commercials are big business.

---

*With apologies, we will be using "he" and "his" for lack of a better pronoun, to avoid the cumbersome "he or she."

- Last year food manufacturers spent over $654 million for commercials about processed cereals, $389 million on soft drinks, and $405 million on gums and candies.
- More money is spent on food commercials than on commercials for automobiles, toilet goods, or even brand-name drugs.
- Between January and October of 1990, 100 new cereals and 1,400 new snacks directed at kids were introduced. All of them are advertised as tasting delicious.

What these slick ads don't tell you is that the reason their foods are so taste-tempting is that they are loaded with fats, salt, sugar, and/or countless unpronounceable chemical additives. If they are rich in fat, most likely they are the types of fats that are putting millions of our children at increased risk of heart disease and early death. In fact, around the age of 20, some 70 percent of our population has begun to develop coronary artery disease.

If we're going to protect our children's health and maximize their potential, then we're going to have to change the way they *think* about food. A good way to do that is to teach them at a very early age about the difference between nutritional foods and the foods that can be unhealthy for them. We can't rely on our schools. Only 300 out of 17,000 high schools offer any courses on nutrition. So nutrition education is up to you.

The Eating For A's Program can be your guide because it is based not on theory but on successful results. The changes that we saw in children like Ricky are not just the observations of individual scientists or researchers but have also been seen in large school populations. Here are two examples.

NEW YORK CITY

In 1977, Elizabeth Cagan was appointed to the New York City school food program after it was criticized by *The New York Times* as having one of the least appetizing breakfast and school lunch programs in the country. She invited experts from universities and colleges as well as advocates on nutrition and health from the area to meet regularly for nearly one year to recommend improvements in the menus. Their recommendations, and especially those of the Nutrition Education and Training Coordinator, Barbara Friedlander Meyer, were implemented in a 3-phase program beginning in 1979. By 1983, according to published university studies, these dietary changes contributed to one of the largest gains in standardized test scores in American history.

What were the changes that Mrs. Cagan and Mrs. Meyer implemented?

First, they dramatically reduced all sources of refined white sugar in the meals. These simply supplied unnecessary "empty calories"—calories devoid of vitamins, minerals, and other nutrients needed for growth and health.

Second, all foods containing artificial colors and flavors were eliminated.

Third, they put a limit on the amount and type of food preservatives allowed in the processed foods they used. Some preservatives had been shown to cause undesirable behavior, such as hyperactivity and restlessness.

And *fourth*, they discovered that the nutritional standards for the National School Lunch Program were inadequate and outdated; as a result, they raised the U.S. Department of Agriculture's RDA (Recommended Daily Allowances) of vitamins and minerals for the entire New York City school program.

They also discovered that there were other school food

programs which reported that more nutritious meals had had a dramatic effect on academic *and* athletic performance.

HELIX HIGH SCHOOL

A good example of one of these programs can be found in the dietary changes effected by Gina Larson, the cafeteria manager of Helix High School, near San Diego, California. In April of 1962, Food Editor Susan Delight of the *San Diego Union* had heard from parents, educators, and others about a meal program that seemed to contribute to the remarkable success of students in the classroom and on the playing field.

She reported that football players, track runners, swimmers, baseball and basketball players all rushed to the special lunch lines every noon at the school's cafeteria to devour meals and salad bar items freshly prepared by Mrs. Larson's staff. Many believed that her meals contributed to Helix High's winning in virtually every sport in California athletic competitions. In addition, year after year, minor injuries among athletes were reduced to less than 30 percent of what they had been before Mrs. Larson took over. Broken bones had been virtually eliminated!

Equally important, the students were near the top academically of every high school grade level in the entire state. The rate of college admission of Helix High School seniors was in the top percentile in the state. Mrs. Larson's diet was so effective that the American Nutrition Society selected Helix High as their pilot school, or model.

Because the students were consistently feeling and performing better, they did not protest when Gina Larson eliminated all foods containing sugar from the menus, as well as candy and other sweets from the snack machines. By demonstrating to youngsters that they felt better when they avoided empty-calorie snacks, and teaching them, as Mrs. Larson said, "to keep their bodies and brains in training," her program had a far-reaching effect not only on the students but also on the school and the surrounding community.

In short, it doesn't matter whether one mother like Phyllis changes Ricky's diet, or a cafeteria manager like Gina Larson changes a high school menu, or a chief administrator like Elizabeth Cagan revamps a breakfast and lunch program serving 600,000 children daily—the results are the same. When children are fed nutritionally dense foods, their potential is maximized and their scholastic and athletic performances are improved.

How Well Do Your Children Eat?

If you're like most parents, you believe that your children are well fed. They're healthy to look at and often have bursts of exuberant energy. A feast of food choices is offered to them from one of the world's most abundantly endowed countries. If anything, many children might seem too well fed because they are hefty for their age.

Therefore it's not too difficult to understand how a 1989 Boston University study could conclude that 11 million students 6 to 17 are "fat." We assume that these children are eating too much. As we know, being overweight is a national problem. If adults are overweight, why wouldn't their children be?

The term *fat*, however, when applied this way, is more dangerous than being overweight. It's defined as being a full 30 percent above ideal weight. To understand this better, we might picture a man who should weigh 180 pounds walking around at 240 pounds. Everything he does will require more effort, taxing his heart to work much harder. Children who are in this category will be especially prone to developing cardiovascular disease by adulthood.

And what about those children who aren't fat or even overweight? A 1989 American Medical Association report concluded that:

- Two-thirds of the 46 million schoolchildren have a cholesterol count above the desired cholesterol level of 140 to 150.
- The poor physical stamina of schoolchildren is reflected in the latest national exercise tests. Only 32 percent of the students achieved scores rated satisfactory. Many children cannot do even one sit-up or chin-up.

  Recent university studies have shown that:
- 40 percent of children aged 5 to 8 have at least one heart disease risk factor. Of these, 60 percent suffer from one or more of the following:

  - high blood pressure
  - high cholesterol levels
  - low physical activity levels

It's increasingly clear that there's a direct relationship between children's diets and their school performance and health. If your child has a high cholesterol count, the Eating For A's Program is designed to lower it. When combined with a regular exercise schedule, Eating for A's will develop the muscular stamina required for any athletic activity. The program achieves this by replacing nonnutritional "empty calorie" foods with those that will fortify your child's body and brain.

But the question of our children's health still remains. In this age of workout videotapes and a 300 million-dollar health and fitness boom, how could our kids be so out of shape? The answer is simple: life-style and diet.

The typical child usually begins his day by eating one of the heavily advertised sugar-laden cereals, with milk. Some don't even bother to eat breakfast. Then he rides to school instead of walking, and so he doesn't get any exercise. He sits in classes all morning long until lunchtime. And to compound it, physical education classes may be offered only twice a week at school.

If the school food program is typical, it offers high-fat, heavily salted and sugared foods. It has the *potential* to offer much more healthful meals, but because the government has warehouses filled with surplus goods purchased from farmers, the schools have become dumping grounds for high-fat whole milk, high-fat meats, and high-fat cheese. High-fat foods are given to the schools free, but the low-fat varieties must be paid for.

Some students use their lunch money for snacks that are offered in vending machines or student-operated canteens. These snacks are of the lowest nutritional quality. For example, children and teenagers now drink 6 times more soda than milk. In fact, the average teenager drinks close to 1,000 twelve-ounce cans of soda a year, or nearly three cans a day.

After lunch, there may be recess, so that a child is encouraged to be overly active immediately after eating. Then he spends the rest of his day sitting in classes. After a bus or car ride home from school, he plops down on the couch to do homework or watch TV. (With the introduction of cable television, a child has forty channels to choose from.) While doing so, he'll probably indulge in a gooey "after-school treat." If it's close enough to dinnertime, he may later complain he has "no appetite."

After dinner, more television, and then to bed. Kids on the average watch 6 hours of TV daily. The equivalent, for their parents, would be to watch 3 full-length movies every day.

Many children don't even eat meals with their families anymore. Some parents are just too busy to prepare meals because of after-work related activities, and few children possess the skills to properly nourish themselves. Some of them simply reach for the easiest-to-eat snack in the refrigerator.

Therefore, what we see in this child is that he eats too many fats and sweets and is not getting enough exercise. It would never occur to us that this child is *malnourished* because it doesn't fit our image of the word.

Overconsumptive Malnutrition

Television informs us constantly that a significant portion of the world lives in chronic hunger. We see children with blindness (xerophthalmia) caused by lack of vitamin A, or pellagra from lack of vitamin B_3. What we do not see is that some of our own children are also malnourished. Even though they eat a lot, much of the food has little or no nutritional value.

Nutrition-poor meals have created a new food phenomenon: *overconsumptive malnutrition*. A half century ago, a number of nutritional scientists warned us about the increasing supply of *denatured and processed food*. They wondered how a food that had 50 nutrients to begin with and, after refining and processing, was left with 7, and then "fortified" with 5 more, could be better than if it had remained untouched. But the food industry won out, and today many individuals believe that a "fortified" food is better than the original.

Of course, much less was known in the 1930s about the body's complex nutritional needs. Zinc, for example, was not even identified as an essential nutrient until 1966. Since then, scientists have identified zinc as important to virtually every enzyme reaction that occurs in the brain. Yet today, because of antiquated fortification regulations, no company that removes zinc from food is required to put it back.

Moreover, many refined foods have high levels of fat, salt, and sweets designed to instantly satisfy our taste buds. Children believe that what tastes good *is* good. This perception is fostered by the food chemists and processors who are constantly perfecting the "right" sensory stimulation with additives. And since whatever children eat must look, taste, and feel right, many chemical additives are required.

People assume that whatever is sold in a supermarket must have some kind of nutritional value. Wouldn't "experts" prohibit the sale of foods that are dangerous to our health? In fact, many favorite items might not even be considered food at all because they cannot be classified into the following traditional four groups:

- fruits and vegetables
- bread and cereals
- meat, fish, and poultry
- milk, cheese, and other dairy products

There is an intrinsic flaw in classifying foods in this way, because where would you place: Desserta, Jell-O, Cremora, Twinkies, Ding Dongs, Tang, Kool-Aid, soft drinks, Doritos, or Moon Pies? Actually these are nonfoods, examples of the source of much of our overconsumptive malnutrition. How are we to understand what these foods are? Certainly we can't explain them by reading the labels. In fact, the labels contain names that are unpronounceable. What we can understand, however, is what we can see with our eyes: specifically, the results of overconsumptive malnutrition that express themselves in a child's "problems."

Do your children have difficulty sleeping? Do they suffer from recurring bad dreams? During the course of dinner, do they suddenly become argumentative? Do they complain that they have muscle pains and can't understand why? Is it difficult for them to get up in the morning even after a full night's sleep? Do they seem to have less energy and less physical stamina when bike riding or playing sports than they did a year ago? Do a number of teachers report that they don't pay attention in class, or that they have difficulty concentrating on the subject? And at times, for no reason, do they suddenly become uncontrollable? We assume our children are just "moody" or "going through a phase," that they're experiencing "behavior changes" or "acting out." We always assume that a child's *thinking is at fault*. They're not self-disciplined enough or self-controlled, or they're too willful. But we forget how thinking, as a function of the brain, is connected to diet.

The Diet-Brain Connection

Imagine a sunny Sunday; you've gone to the woods with your family. You've brought a picnic basket, but somehow it's been lost. In searching for it, you and your family also become lost. You can't find your way back to the trail. The children begin to get hungry and thirsty, and you realize that you are, too. You feel tired and decide to sit down and think your way out of the situation.

Which organ of your body do you suppose is first affected by this sudden lack of food?

The answer is the brain.

Through a series of breakthrough discoveries, the work of scientists has confirmed that in humans *the first organ to suffer from temporary malnutrition is the brain*.

Most of us assume that the brain is separate from the rest of the body. We associate *thinking* with the brain, *feeling* with the heart, and *hunger* with the stomach. The brain, however, is responsible for all *three* functions. In addition, it determines and influences the regulation of at least one thousand other metabolic (chemical) processes occurring every second we live.

Our overall behavior, memory, and moods are controlled by the brain. So is our concentration and our ability to think calmly, which are the keys to learning. Although the brain is only 2 percent of the body's weight, it utilizes at least 20 percent of the body's energy sources. No other organ is so demanding. And the tremendous energy required by the brain is entirely affected by what we eat.

Therefore, when you and your family become hungry in the woods, it's because the brain is sending messages that it needs food to continue working. If your hunger persists, your brain experiences an "energy shortage." At that point, the limbic system—the most primitive part of the brain—has the priority on the available energy. This is because the limbic system controls the involuntary muscle responses, like breathing and pumping blood. So the regions that don't get enough energy are those that contribute to reasoning and thinking.

Imagine, then, a nutrient-poor diet that continues daily for years on end. There are too few brain nutrients to allow the brain to function at peak performance. In children, all sorts of "psychological problems" seem to pop up. They might be easily frustrated and grow angry, or remain timid and shy. They might be easily distracted, or have erratic energy. They might have trouble remembering things that happened a little while ago, or seem overly active for no reason.

While many things can contribute to a child's athletic and academic performance and his behavior, we must look first in the most obvious place of all: the daily diet.

How Intelligent Are Your Children?

If you're like most parents, you have a clear idea of how smart your children are. Your opinion might be formed from your own observation, their IQ tests, grade scores, and their teachers' remarks. Teachers often say that children aren't "living up to their full potential," or that they're "smarter than their grades" and should "apply themselves more to their schoolwork." Recent statistics seem to confirm these observations.

- The National Assessment of Educational Progress Report, developed by the U.S. Department of Education, concluded that over the past 20 years the performance of students "is low and not improving."

Other statistics confirm these observations:

- In the areas of math, science, and reading, the United States now ranks twentieth among the developed countries.
- The nation's college admissions test scores, based on the SAT exams, have declined for the past 25 years.
- Nationally, illiteracy and the high school drop-out rate are at an all-time high.

We constantly read that our educational system has to be overhauled. More money has to be poured into the renovation of schools. Teachers must be better trained and paid higher salaries. There should be smaller classes and longer hours with more emphasis placed on homework. Children should be made to watch less television, read more, and pay more attention to schoolwork. All of these suggestions are valid, to a degree. What nobody ever emphasizes, however, is that *our children should be fed to be smarter!*

A nutritious diet increases any child's potential to use his given intelligence. Yet, when a child is being tested, have you ever heard a teacher or psychologist ask: "What did you eat this morning?"

When intelligence tests are taken there are never any questions such as: What do you eat for lunch at school? What are your favorite snack foods? What did you eat just before you took this exam?

We never ask such questions because we assume that intelligence is like a flame. It burns naturally and brightly of its own accord, like a candle feeding on air. But if there's not enough air in the room, the candle flame begins to sputter. And the diet of American children, on the whole, is like a room with too little air to support the flame.

Your children have never been tested after weeks of eating meals rich in learning nutrients. They have never embarked on a meal program designed to enhance their intelligence to the fullest. And once they do, the Eating For A's Program can change their lives. The guidelines in this book will serve your children into their teenage years and beyond. This is a 12-week program for change, and a maintenance program for life.

2

THE CORNERSTONE
OF LEARNING

The School District Special Advisement Committee was unsure what to do with Clarence. His teachers had asked the committee to remove him from school and recommend him for special education services. The general assessment was he was either in need of psychological counseling or involved with drugs or alcohol. He couldn't keep his mind on classwork and never seemed to settle down. When a teacher was talking, Clarence spoke with other students. He impulsively got up out of his seat, and didn't do the work assigned on the blackboard. His homework was handed in only sporadically.

When he was referred to Alexander Schauss for testing, he was given the Wechsler Intelligence Scale for Children—Revised (WISC—R). His initial IQ score was in the mid-90s, the "low normal" range, which explained his below-average performance and D grades. During the test, Clarence had difficulty following instructions. Even when the instructions were read to him, he seemed resistant to following directions.

He got up out of his chair often and chatted frequently. When asked, "What did you have for breakfast this morning?" he said, "I never eat breakfast."

In most cases, once such tests were completed and prepared as a report, the matter would have ended with the evaluator's recommendation. Luckily, however, Alexander Schauss knew Clarence personally. The boy came from a hardworking family and had a good relationship with both his parents. He also seemed brighter than his test results indicated, so Schauss wrote a letter to his parents asking that Clarence be retested in three weeks. Attached to the letter was a list of recommended meals and snacks, with breakfast emphasized and underlined in red ink. The letter was followed up with phone calls stressing that the diet instructions be followed closely. "He gets up too late to eat breakfast," Clarence's mother said. "And besides, he's not hungry in the morning."

Alexander Schauss emphasized the importance of nutrient foods at the start of the day and suggested an earlier bedtime for Clarence.

Three weeks later, Clarence was tested again. His IQ registered in the mid-120s, a *27.5-point rise!* It was the largest increase Schauss had seen since his initial training in psychometric and intelligence testing at the University of New Mexico. An IQ in the mid-120s established that Clarence could be a top student. His father also mentioned, "When I was driving him here in the car, he was much less restless. All this week he's been less moody."

In a short follow-up session with his parents, a school counselor, two teachers, and a school psychologist, everyone commented on Clarence's significant improvement. He was calmer and consistently listened to his teachers. He watched much less television and spent more time outside playing with his neighborhood friends. The teachers were particularly interested in knowing what Clarence's parents had done to help him.

Before we explain how breakfast could account for such an improvement, it is important to stress that Clarence's story is "anecdotal evidence." Parents should not expect such dramatic results just because their children are using Eating For A's breakfast recipes. Even though several other students referred to Alexander Schauss also showed similar substantial improvements, excellent results in a small number of cases do not constitute strong scientific evidence in and of themselves.

However, it has been well documented that a child's learning ability and brain development can be increased substantially by a number of factors—and a good diet is one of them. Scientists have found that IQ's will rise in schoolchildren if they are given nutrient supplements, particularly those children with poor diets. Children whose diets were low in vitamins and minerals seemed to benefit most from nutritional supplements. There are some reported cases where diet supplements resulted in improved IQ scores even more dramatic than Clarence's. Other factors, such as environmental stimulation, genetics, psychological stress, and a history of positive or negative reinforcement ("You're so smart!" or "You're so dumb!") also play an important part.

The change in Clarence, however, was more than just 27.5 test points. The new eating pattern seemed to help him begin a new life. When Clarence had first arrived for testing, he hadn't eaten anything since the night before. Without realizing it, the boy was literally *fasting every day until lunchtime.* This daily denial of nutrients impaired his brain's delicate chemical equilibrium. If a child's chemistry is "off," either due to stress or inadequate diet, no amount of prodding will force him to "stay on task," as teachers say. This was obvious in Clarence's inability to follow instructions and sit still—

behavior problems he demonstrated daily in class. After three weeks, his brain had been receiving a daily supply of learning nutrients, particularly in the morning. Given his history, it isn't really so surprising that Clarence showed such a marked improvement in behavior and test scores. His brain was suddenly provided with the fuel that enabled it to concentrate.

What Is Concentration?

Essentially, concentration is the mind's ability to control its attention span. When a child attempts to learn, a number of factors come into play. His native intelligence, the amount of sleep he's had, the classroom environment, and the teacher's skill are all vital. But the most important source of concentration is the *chemical equilibrium* of the brain. If a child's chemistry is unbalanced, his mind will "wander" no matter how much he tries to apply himself—his brain is receiving sensory messages that divert his attention.

Every single second our brains are receiving thousands of requests from its cells to provide information. These requests come in the form of electrical messages from the nervous system. The brain's job is to sort through these messages and find the right response for each of them. And the orders your child's brain dispatches are very diverse. It tells your child's muscles to contract, his heart to pump faster, his eyes to focus, his ears to listen, his lungs to keep breathing, and his stomach to secrete enzymes for digestion. At the same time, and all the time, it's sending messages to every corner of his body to keep him growing taller, stronger, healthier, smarter, and more inquisitive.

With all of this mental activity constantly going on, a child's brain must be calm in order to concentrate. A calm brain is one that is not overwhelmed by a flood of thoughts.

Instead, it can listen to itself think, and therefore attend to the process of thoughts involved in answering a question. And the key to good concentration is the chemical equilibrium established by diet: specifically, the 12 learning nutrients that are the substance and source of the Eating For A's Program.

The Twelve Learning Nutrients

The nutrients that we are talking about are all vitamins and minerals. They not only contribute to regulating our body's metabolism but also assist in the processes that release energy quickly from digested food. Vitamins are a group of potent organic compounds other than fat, protein, or carbohydrates that are necessary for the body's maintenance and growth. They differ from hormones, which have similar benefits, in that they must be supplied by diet. Minerals are naturally occurring elements found in the earth. They belong to two groups: macro (bulk) minerals and micro (trace) minerals. The seven *macronutrients* account for most of the minerals in our body. Calcium and phosphorus, required in bone formation, are two good examples. *Micronutrients* are needed in much smaller amounts, but some of them, such as *zinc* or *iron*, play a major role in almost every biochemical activity the brain performs. The following description shows how they are related to the Eating For A's Program.

VITAMINS

VITAMIN A

Benefits: Helps in the manufacturing of protein and DNA.

Deficiency effects: Depression and apathy. In infants, retarded brain growth.

THIAMIN (VITAMIN B$_1$)

Benefits: Helps the brain process energy from glucose and proteins.

Deficiency effects: Fatigue, impaired memory, mental confusion, conduct disorder, irritability, impulsiveness, poor sleep.

RIBOFLAVIN (VITAMIN B$_2$)

Benefits: Helps maintain the nerve's myelin (a substance that coats the nerve and helps it conduct information), assists in making energy available to the brain.

Deficiency effects: Impairs the growth of the brain in young children and contributes to behavior problems.

NIACIN (VITAMIN B$_3$)

Benefits: Helps the brain produce essential chemicals; aids in the manufacture of protein.

Deficiency effects: Irritability, fatigue, poor concentration, mood swings, poor sleep.

PYRIDOXINE (VITAMIN B$_6$)

Benefits: Helps the brain produce essential chemicals; aids in the manufacturing of protein.

Deficiency effects: Irritability, fatigue, poor concentration, mood swings, poor sleep, poor memory.

FOLIC ACID

Benefits: Helps produce RNA/DNA—both important in the formation of nucleic acids and in the storage of recent memory events.

Deficiency effects: Apathy, impaired memory, irritability, withdrawal, slowing of all intellectual processes.

VITAMIN C

Benefits: Helps in the utilization of protein; improves absorption of certain forms of iron needed by the brain.

Deficiency effects: Fatigue, depression, hypersensitivity.

MINERALS

IRON

Benefits: Assists in the processing of nutrients required in brain activity; helps process neurotransmitters and DNA.

Deficiency effects: Conduct disorder, inattentiveness, hyperactivity, poor concentration.

MAGNESIUM

Benefits: Helps get energy from nutrients for the brain.

Deficiency effects: Irritability, nervousness, lethargy, depression, confusion.

POTASSIUM

Benefits: Required for normal levels of brain neurotransmitters (chemicals that allow information to pass from one brain circuit to another).

Deficiency effects: Feelings of weakness, loss of appetite, nausea, irrational thinking, confusion.

ZINC

Benefits: Required in virtually every enzyme reaction in the brain; helps manufacture RNA, DNA, and protein; helps provide energy from glucose and protein.

Deficiency effects: Lethargy, irritability, poor eating habits, poor appetite, anorexia, fatigue, confusion.

CHROMIUM

Benefits: Essential for glucose metabolism (the human brain is almost totally dependent on glucose for its fuel).

Deficiency effects: Poor concentration, impaired short-term memory, mood fluctuation, general feelings of tiredness.

The following diagram shows the increased percentage of the Eating for A's 12 learning nutrients above the government's recommended daily allowance (RDA) standards. Our program is not interested in "minimum" requirements for children but rather amounts that will enable them to maximize their potential.

EATING FOR A's
PERCENTAGE INCREASE OVER U.S. RDA's

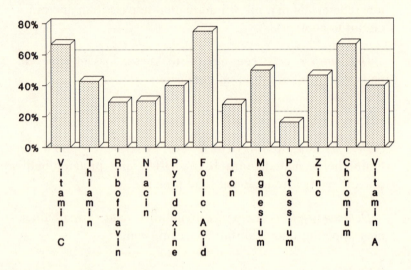

IRON DEFICIENCY

I ron deficiency is believed to be the most prevalent world-wide nutritional deficiency and the most frequent cause of anemia. According to numerous studies, it is the most common deficiency in American, Canadian, British, and Australian children.

Iron plays an important role in brain function. In children who have inadequate iron levels in the brain, cognitive processing may be impaired. Cognitive activities in the brain occur primarily in the left hemisphere which governs right-hand control, spoken language, number skills, written language, scientific skills, and reasoning.

The behavioral problems associated with lack of iron have been reported for two decades. Dr. Frank Oski, currently chairman of the Department of Pediatrics at Johns Hopkins University, has conducted studies showing that

young adolescents with iron deficiency anemia have significantly lower scores on school achievement tests than
nonanemic students.

Another study found that conduct problems in the classroom were far more frequent among anemic than nonanemic students. Iron-deficient students exhibited restlessness and irritable and disruptive behavior. In those
students who had the poorest iron levels, it was found that
their behavioral patterns reached such levels of severity as
to impair their ability to learn.

IRON AND VITAMIN C

The behavioral problems associated with lack of iron
have been reported for two decades. Other researchers
at The Rockefeller University and the University of Colorado
have found that the motivation to persist in intellectually
challenging tasks is lower, that the attention span is shorter,
and that overall intellectual performance is diminished in
iron-deficient children.

A good example of iron's effect on brain functioning was
demonstrated in a 14-year-old boy placed in special education due to disruptive behavior and poor academic performance. A careful evaluation of his diet revealed a poor
intake of iron-rich foods. Bloods tests confirmed that he was
nearly iron deficient. Instead of giving him vitamin pills
rich in iron, his parents were instructed to increase the iron-
rich foods that he liked, combined with vitamin C rich foods
and beverages.

Vitamin C changes the form of iron found in nonanimal
sources, such as grains or vegetables, known as *nonheme*
iron, to a much better absorbed form called heme iron.
When a sufficient supply of vitamin C is consumed with a
diet adequate in nonheme iron, the vitamin C modifies the
iron, and makes it more readily absorbable. This is of
particular importance for those who are on vegetarian
diets.

You might have seen that many deficiency effects are the same for more than one nutrient. For instance, irritability can be a result of too little thiamin (B_1), pyridoxine (B_6), folic acid, magnesium, and zinc. This is an excellent example of the holistic nature of the body. You cannot treat an ailment or a deficiency with only one vitamin or only one food. Your child could be eating foods with adequate quantities of B_1, B_6, folic acid, and magnesium, but because he was low in zinc, he might still exhibit signs of irritability.

Fortunately, when you are feeding the mind properly, you are also nourishing the rest of the body. And vice versa. So, although we call these learning nutrients for the brain, they are nutrients for the entire child as well.

Which Kinds of Foods Contain These Nutrients?

The foods highest in brain nutrients are what most of us think of as "basic" foods—good bread, fresh fruit and vegetables, fish, etc. They are also sometimes referred to as "natural foods." Doesn't this sound easy? All you have to do is go out and buy these foods, serve them to your family, and wait for your child to get smarter, behave better, and become an all-around athlete. Right?

Wrong!

First, you need to find out something about food in general. For example, take this short quiz.

The kind of food I buy is *mostly* determined by:

1. The consumer (me)
2. The store manager
3. The food manufacturer's advertising agency
4. The food manufacturer
5. The government

6. The farmer
7. The food manufacturer's chemist

The answer is 7. Surprised? Most of our food supply is adulterated. This means that things like artificial colorings and flavorings, preservatives, and conditioners are added to foods by the chemists who work for food companies.

WHAT IS NATURAL?

The term *natural* is applied to a whole range of foods, but it is often misused. *Natural* should mean that the food is as close to nature as possible. Ideally, this is why we eat food— for the *life* it contains. And natural food has a life force, which in turn nourishes our own life force. When a food is adulterated with chemical additives, its life force is altered. Simply stated, it is not as good for your body or your mind.

Unfortunately, in today's diet where there is a predominance of fast foods, "junk" foods, and highly processed foods, these brain nutrients are often missing or are found in such small quantities as to be inadequate.

PROCESSED FOOD

Processed food often contains excessive amounts of salt, sugar, and chemical additives in the form of preservatives, artificial coloring, and flavorings, etc. Sometimes, as in the case of bleached white bread, some nutrients are even eliminated. Or, a food is so highly processed that it no longer contains any element of the original food. Example: The popular "shakes" sold in most fast-food establishments contain no milk; rather they are mostly chemicals and sugar.

Processed food often has vitamin fortification. This means that after the nutrients are removed from the food, an attempt is made to put them back in the form of a vitamin tablet. Unfortunately, once something in its natural state has been removed, no amount of laboratory sophistication can put it back the same way. Some people may say, "So what? We still get the vitamins." We strongly disagree.

FORTIFICATION

As an example of how elaborately confusing fortification can be, let us examine bread products. Which form of iron is used to "fortify" your bread loaf? If it's *ferrous sulfate*, that's fine, since its bioavailability (availability to the body) is good. But if it's *ferric orthophosphate* or *sodium iron pyrophosphate*, these are *poorly absorbed* by the body. Processors could use iron sources whose bioavailability is that of ferrous sulfate, like *ferrous gluconate, ferric ammonium citrate, or ferrous fumarate*, but these are *not economically practical* for the fortification of flour.

Then there is the amount of iron needed to truly reintroduce the level of iron originally present in the wheat grains prior to processing. When the higher preprocessed iron levels are added to flour, they affect the bread quality and "loaf volume" because they react with a commonly used dough conditioner, *potassium bromate* (recently suspected of being a kidney carcinogen in rats). Also, iron tends to "oxidize," meaning it can turn gray or black, producing little dark spots in the dough—not something bakers want.

Therefore, only by using *much less iron* than we might need are these problems resolved. There are many other problems in food fortification that keep the food technologists and chemists very busy devising and "improving" processed foods. Wouldn't it simply be better to eat a food, such as wheat bread, that has been minimally processed?

In addition, we should remember that for all their knowledge of chemical structures, scientists have yet to create an apple in a laboratory. They have yet to create fruits that contain seeds or bear other fruit. Instead, we are offered cheese that isn't cheese, meat laced with antibiotics, and potential cancer-causing agents in a wide variety of the foods displayed on every supermarket shelf.

ADDITIVES AND YOUR CHILD

The use of artificial colorings and flavorings is of particular importance where children are concerned. *Why?* The most important reason is that children differ from adults in terms of their body mass. Adults can more safely absorb certain chemicals because their bodies are so much larger, denser, and stronger.

Your child is consuming far more artificial colorings and flavorings than you realize. In fact, most artificially colored food is produced for children because they are naturally drawn to bright colors. Inevitably, they will reach for colored cereals, candies, and snacks, and consequently, they're eating more adulterated, chemically laden foods than nutritious ones. Could your children be sensitive to these artificial colors and flavors? And if they are, how can you know?

Most chemical food additives are derived from coal-tar petroleum, to which some children are allergic. Reactions to coal tar petroleum usually include:

- hives
- nasal congestion
- edema
- gastrointestinal reactions
- headaches
- lethargy
- eczema

They also cause measurable changes in behavior and motor functioning.

Additives are not limited to flavoring, coloring, or preservative agents. Some are believed essential in order to maintain the vast food supply found in our supermarkets. Pesticide residues may be found on many fruits and vegetables. An apple, for example, sits on a shelf, rosy, shining, and appealing. It looks so natural, but is it? No, it's probably been grown with artificial fertilizer, sprayed with pesticides, stored for many months under special temperature conditions, and waxed to maintain its shelf life and good looks. Fortunately, as more consumers become nutritionally aware, more supermarkets and health foods stores are carrying pesticide-free apples and other fruits.

Meats and poultry can produce adverse reactions in some people as a result of contaminated feed given to animals and fowl. Other people are sensitive to the fumigants sprayed on dried fruits and nuts, or to the bleaches used to whiten flour, or to the ethylene gas residues used to artificially ripen fruit (like bananas) after distribution to retailers. Still others are sensitive to the potassium metasulfites sprayed on salads and potatoes to prevent spoilage while maintaining the appearance of crispness, or to the fungicides used on crates before shipping citrus fruits.

The list of reactive chemicals in our food and water supply grows longer every year. Although it is still not known what causes such reactions in some people but not in others, it is clear that the avoidance of as many of these substances as possible is prudent.

Among the most common brain reactions to food additives are:

- drowsiness
- headaches
- excess motor activity
- disorientation
- faintness
- fatigue
- insomnia
- disorganized thinking
- mood swings
- lack of concentration

How common these problems are remains unknown. Of the more than 65,000 chemicals that we are exposed to in our air, water, and food, less than 1 percent have been adequately tested for their effects on our brain and nervous system.

WHAT ABOUT GOVERNMENT REGULATION?

Surely, the government wouldn't allow manufacturers to put something harmful into the food, would it?

The government does not do so wittingly. The FDA (Food and Drug Administration), which is the governmental agency responsible for food safety, publishes a GRAS (Generally Recommended as Safe) list every year. All the chemical additives on this list are permissible. The problem is that often, after a few years or further testing, certain items are removed from the list because they have been found to be harmful (for example: cause cancer). You can take your chances and go along with the GRAS list. But we strongly believe in erring on the side of safety by choosing foods that contain few or no chemicals—particularly as most of these additives are there so that the food will look good or last longer and not because they will enhance our well-being.

For example, several years ago, the Office of School Food and Nutrition Services of the New York City Board of Education decided to change its food specifications and, among other things, eliminate nonbeneficial additives and preservatives. Shortly thereafter, a whole cadre of chemists from the Kellogg's cereal company descended and practically accused the office of endangering the health of the one million children who ate breakfast in the school district. Their argument was that BHT and BHA (common preservatives found in cereals) prevented cereals from going rancid. When questioned about why these preservatives were necessary, they replied that the cereals were packaged for a 2-year shelf life. Two years! Some people don't even keep clothes that long.

When Kellogg's was informed that it would lose the New York City account if it did not remove the additives, the chemists returned to their labs—and *voilà!* Cereal without BHA or BHT. A further benefit: once having established that it was all right to remove these additives, the company began supplying the same cereal—minus the BHA and BHT—to the general public.

SUGAR-RICH JUNK FOODS

Junk foods, in addition to containing the additives mentioned above, usually are so-named because they contain too much sugar (or other forms of empty calorie sweeteners such as dextrose, corn syrup, maltose), salt, or fat. (See label information on p. 77 for a complete list.)

In regard to the Eating For A's Program, the most serious argument against sugar is that it is not a food with any nutritive value. Children tend to eat foods high in sugar and seem to have been born with a "sweet tooth" (not so unlikely considering the first thing most infants get in the hospital after birth is sugar water!). So, in addition to not deriving any nutrition, they are preventing themselves from getting nutrition from other foods because they are filling themselves up with sugar. Sugar calories are empty calories.

A food is described as being "empty calorie" because the calories it contains produce energy (and eventually weight gain) without adding any nutrition. Sugar, in particular, gets into the bloodstream quickly. The result is a sudden burst of energy, caused by a quick rise in the blood sugar level. The high level doesn't last, however, but instead is quickly dissipated. And when this happens, the blood sugar level actually goes lower than it was before. In order to keep from being fatigued, the body then needs more sugar.

This is one of the reasons eating sugary foods can become habit-forming. Without being conscious of it, children want more—the more they have, the more they want—and most of them cannot control their intake. Recent studies show that sugar affects children differently and more adversely than adults in terms of their learning ability and behavior (attention span, irritability, etc.).

One of the most common junk foods is carbonated, flavored soda. The main ingredient in sodas is sugar, with artificial colorings and flavorings. Clearly, any program that aims to eliminate junk foods must also take a hard line on soda, and the Eating For A's Program gives a range of alternative drinks.

LEARNING ABOUT NUTRIENT FOODS

Now, with this background information, we are ready to look at the foods rich in the 12 learning nutrients. A list of them is provided on pp. 26–29. You'll be able to refer to it throughout the program. Before beginning the program, you might want to appraise the overall health of your child. The next chapter tells you how to do this.

3

SPECIAL DIETARY CONSIDERATIONS

Before beginning this program, it is important that you be attuned to your child's overall health and well-being. Are there specific dietary considerations that apply to your child? Do certain minor health problems keep recurring? This chapter details some common symptoms that may relate to your child's diet and offers advice about what to do if you notice telltale signs.

Food and Chemical Allergies

Allergies are one of the immune system's responses to unfamiliar substances. The body sets up a defensive reaction to foods it cannot digest, and it becomes sensitive to them in ways that are symptomatic. For example, excessive ear infections, colic, or constant nasal congestion are often signs of food allergies and should not be dismissed.

In an ironic stroke of nature, it is often the craving for a particular food that is an excellent indication of an allergy to it. Children, of course, crave particular foods constantly— but food allergies are a lot more common than we realize. In Chapter 2, we discussed our general concerns regarding artificial food colorings, flavorings, and preservatives. If there is an outright allergy to these chemicals, it can cause a variety of brain reactions that can interfere with a child's mental and physical performance. We must, therefore, review some of the characteristic signs associated with allergies. These signs have been studied for more than 30 years by Dr. Doris Rapp, a leading pediatric allergist. She has identified both the behavioral and physiological indications, the majority of which are seen above the neck. The following are some of the most common manifestations.

Eyes: Look for dark circles or "shiners" under the eyes, or deep wrinkles which may appear just below the skin of the eye or on the lower eyelid. At times, the eyelids may appear swollen or puffy; tiny white scales may appear on the eyelashes. Some children have two puffy areas—one directly below the eye and the other a rounded bulge just below the outer edge of the eye in the region above the cheeks. Sometimes, the eyes get watery or "glassy" just before and during the period of unusual motor activity or changes in behavior. Watery, itchy, red eyes are typical allergic reactions.

Nose: Note whether your child has frequent nasal stuffiness or watery, runny nasal secretions. If the nose is frequently stuffy and running, the child tends to rub it with the back of his hand in an upward motion. Eventually, this can cause a small half wrinkle just above the tip of the nose—a telltale sign of an allergy.

Earlobes: The earlobes may feel warm to the touch and look very red. In such cases chemicals called phenols should be particularly suspected, although almost any food or chemical could cause this reaction.

Cheeks: Check to see if your child's cheeks suddenly become red with rough patches shortly after eating something.

Lips and Mouth Area: The lips of allergic children often become swollen and puffy, especially the edges, which can appear almost yellowish. In many such children, the lips look as though they have been chewed or bitten. Also look for cracks in the corner or central part of the lip, and observe whether your child licks that area frequently. Sometimes this is a sign of a rare vitamin B_2 deficiency, but more often it's an allergic reaction to a food or to some substance or chemical in the air. Some children and infants constantly lick the entire area around the lips, resulting in a rash. When teenage girls get pimples on the chin (perioral dermatitis) it may be due to a food sensitivity.

In some children, contact with certain toothpaste, food, or even bubble gum has caused similar problems. It's easy to find out, because it will clear up when the offending food or chemical is eliminated.

Face: Although it is rare, in some allergic children the face becomes very pale, almost anemic-looking, as though all the color has been drained out. Deficiencies of iron, folic acid, or B_{12} should be considered, but when they have been corrected and the look still persists, food allergies should be suspected.

Voice: In many children, and even adults, an almost squeaky, high-pitched voice has been associated with various offending substances. Even chronic laryngitis, unclear speech, and intermittent stuttering may be related to a food allergy. Doctors have noticed that hyperactive children who tend to speak a lot but make no sense improve greatly once the offending substance(s) has been identified and eliminated.

Hands: Cold hands (and feet) are common in people with allergies. In children, additionally there is marked eczema and very wrinkled palms.

Body: Many children who perspire profusely have reported that perspiration stopped when they found and eliminated the offending food or chemical. In some children tender spots develop in their skin, like deep localized areas of swelling, even though the surface skin looks normal.

Behavior: Changes in behavior due to food or chemical allergies have been well documented by numerous scientists and pediatric allergists. We have listed some kinds of behavioral problems in the set of questions below. But under no circumstance exclude the possibility that your child may be suffering from some other type of stress, either psychological or physiological. For example: A child with pinworms might have a very hard time falling alseep, or make frequent trips to the bathroom; or a child may exhibit the same behavior if he is trying to cope with a classroom bully, an insensitive teacher, or an abusive parent. Noticeable changes in your child's behavior demand your attention. A poor diet or an allergy may be only one possible explanation. Yet even if your child is faced with serious psychological problems, the Eating For A's Program can help his mind cope with the stress.

Once you have ruled out causes that may be psychological or physiological you may suspect the problem is related to diet. Ask yourself the same questions a pediatric allergist might ask in determining the cause of your child's behavioral problems.

■ Does my child's personality easily change from Dr. Jekyll to Mr. Hyde? If so, was the child eating anything just before the change occurred? If yes, what precisely was he eating?

- Is my child particularly uncontrollable after eating foods associated with Halloween, Easter, Christmas, birthday parties, or other special occasions, like visits to grandparents or relatives?
- Does my child seem excessively thirsty, needing several drinks before finally being able to go to sleep?
- Does my child read well one day and not the next?
- Does my child always crave one particular food and tend to binge on it?
- Are there noticeable changes in my child's handwriting, associated with a deterioration in his behavior?
- Does my child have frequent nightmares or difficulty getting to sleep or staying asleep?

The First Step

What do you do if you suspect your child may have a food or chemical allergy? The first step is to consult a licensed health practitioner who is familiar with a specialist trained in diagnosing and treating such problems. These specialists have the knowledge and experience to identify the offending foods or chemicals most frequently implicated in these types of reactions. If he suspects a chemical sensitivity, the doctor would know which complaints are more typical of chemically sensitive patients.

He might ask such questions as:

- Can you smell odors that others don't?
- Do you get dizzy or nauseated when exposed to the odor of perfumes, tobacco smoke, soft plastics, synthetic carpets, or auto exhaust?

- Do you crave the odor of fresh paint or the smell of a new car?
- Does the odor of your mother's nail polish remover or your father's shoe polish bother you?

Child allergy specialists also know other possible explanations, besides foods and chemicals, which could be causing your child's problems, including house mite excrement (7,000 mites can fit on a dime!), cat or dog dander, nearby industrial gases, or even your home's natural gas or oil burner. The list of possibilities is virtually endless.

THE ELIMINATION DIET

If you are fairly certain that a specific food or foods might be contributing to your child's symptoms, you should try one of the simplest approaches—the elimination diet. This diet is actually a test to discover if the symptoms disappear or abate when a suspect food is not eaten for a period of time. This is the way it works: Completely omit the suspected food (one food at a time) from the diet. Then reintroduce it, in the same quantities as before the test, but *no earlier than three days* after omitting it. If the symptoms disappear during the time when the food was eliminated and reappear upon exposure to it, it is reasonable to suspect that the food was causing the reaction.

Physical symptoms such as *rash, hives, and diarrhea* usually appear soon after reexposure; behavioral reactions are sometimes delayed by many hours, even days, before they are evident. If no symptoms appear within three days, you can assume the food is not an allergen and you can repeat the process with another food. Do this for each suspected food.

In many cases, the elimination diet will reveal to you the

food that is causing your child's problem. When you find the offending food, it is best to avoid it. It is a good idea to consult with a specialist, even if you have successfully identified the food causing the allergy. An expert in the field can explain to you and your child how the offending food or chemical may be hidden in other foods, even though the food is not included on an ingredient list.

For example, did you know that hen's eggs are used in making some root beers, as well as in mayonnaise? Or that cow's milk might be found in common luncheon meats or many canned soups?

The most common foods pediatric allergists report as causing behavioral, emotional, or physiological problems are found in virtually every kitchen:

- cow's milk (and related products such as cheese and cream)
- wheat and products made from it (spaghetti, bread, crackers, etc.)
- hen's eggs
- corn (including corn syrup and even most vitamin C tablets!)
- cocoa and chocolate
- beef, pork
- peanuts
- oranges and grapes
- sugar
- artificial food coloring and preservatives, such as benzoic acid (i.e., sodium benzoate), BHA, BHT, etc.
- soy

An interesting study conducted several years ago found that children allergic to refined sugar (sucrose) reacted only to a specific type of sugar. For example, while some children's behavior became noticeably worse after ingesting cane sugar, other children reacted only to sugar refined from beets or corn. This puts a new twist on the controversy regarding sugar and behavior, because nearly half the children tested were found to react to beet sugar, while the other half reacted to cane sugar. So if your child is sensitive to sugar—is it cane, beet, or corn (sometimes called fructose)?

WHITE SUGAR (SUCROSE)

In recent years there have been a series of studies examining the effects of refined sugar, also known as sucrose, on children's behavior. One, from Yale University's School of Medicine, found hormonal evidence that supports the popular belief that sugar can provoke abnormal behavior in some children. In the study, children given refined sugar experienced levels of adrenaline in their blood ten times higher than they were before they ate the sweet. This led to anxiety, difficulty in concentrating, and crankiness.

Unlike previous studies, the children were given refined white sugar on an empty stomach; other studies gave children sugar *along with* other foods and concluded that the sugar had no effect on behavior. This suggests that children may be at much greater risk of exhibiting abnormal behavior if they eat sugar-rich snacks than if they eat sugar in a dessert following a full meal.

Some children have been found to exhibit antisocial behavior when given *appreciable amounts* of sugar. A series of scientific studies of institutionalized delinquent youths conducted by California State University researchers showed that antisocial behavior can be reduced by nearly half if sugar is restricted to very minimal levels. Substituting nutritious snacks such as fruit, nuts, or cheese makes this possible.

COW'S MILK

Cow's milk warrants special mention because it is an important source of calcium for many children, providing 1,200 milligrams per quart. However, it is also one of the most frequent food allergens and has been shown to cause mental fogginess, lethargy, memory impairment, depression, and hyperactivity. This is in addition to the worldwide problem of milk intolerance. Many children from various ethnic and racial backgrounds are unable to digest the sugar (called "lactose") in milk, due to the absence in their digestive system of an enzyme (called "lactase") whch is specifically designed to break down the lactose. Unless lactose is broken down, they can suffer diarrhea and other discomforts. While less than 10 percent of white Americans, Danes, Swedes, or Swiss have lactose intolerance, more than 50 percent of children and adults from other cultures do. The startling statistics are: Filipinos (90 percent), Thais (90 percent), Bantus (90 percent), Japanese (85 percent), Taiwanese (85 percent), Greek Cypriots (85 percent), Sicilian Italians (85 percent), Eskimos (80 percent); Ashkenazi Jews (78 percent), Arabs (78 percent), Afro-Americans (70 percent), Peruvians (70 percent), Israeli Jews (58 percent), and Indians (50 percent).

Since milk might be a food to be avoided by children of these cultural backgrounds, alternative sources of calcium should be considered. For example, 4 ounces of wheat flour, 1 cup of collard greens, or 3 ounces of sardines provide 250 milligrams of calcium. Other good sources include fish and seafood such as salmon and shrimp, kidney beans, broccoli, soybeans, and almonds. There is medical evidence that even if children take in less than the recommended amount of calcium, the body makes up for it by increasing the absorption of that portion it does receive in the diet. Nutrition researchers also know that a reduction in the intake of animal protein, or replacing animal protein with plant protein, results in improved calcium balance.

RELIEF FROM ALLERGIES

Many children who have an identified food allergy can eat the offending food occasionally, with the result that their symptoms gradually subside or are less severe. One method of doing this is the *4-day rotation diet*. On this diet, no one food is eaten more often than once every 4 days. Over a period of time, without any other treatment, symptoms usually subside. However, this diet may be too great a challenge for most parents and they may want to seek other professional advice. A specialist has ways to build up an immunity to an allergy, such as preparing food extracts and administering them over a period of time.

The Overweight Child

Obesity is an all too common problem in children. Experts who have studied obesity agree that the best treatment for long-term weight loss and maintenance is a combination of nutritional and behavioral approaches. A lifelong exercise program is essential, and this will be discussed in Chapter 9.

Behavioral approaches emphasize looking at the possible causes of non-useful eating habits, while developing and practicing strategies to modify these habits. It is important that there be positive consequences for practicing new and more useful behaviors. For example, a mother knew that her son wanted a toy called Swamp Thing. She struck a bargain with him, explaining, "If you try some new foods together with me for the next three days, Dad and I will buy you Swamp Thing." It worked very well because they were exploring the new foods together, and because her husband was included in buying the gift. If you can find out what your child is eager to have, you can make that a positive consequence of changing his diet.

Here is another example: Your child is always snacking before dinner as he sits watching his favorite afternoon TV show. He may not even be aware that he *is* taking in these extra calories. If he becomes conscious of his behavior, he may begin to restrict his snacking until dinner, thereby cutting out hundreds of needless calories, and feeling more energetic while losing weight. And of course, if he *does* snack, you can provide him with less caloric varieties, examples of which are found throughout this book. In time, you might even enroll him in an after-school exercise activity that utilizes calories and strengthens his entire body.

Your own behavior around your child can have a major effect on his eating habits. Children usually react poorly to their parents' nagging and may do the very opposite of what is wanted. A parent's constant reminder that his child should eat less may actually result in his eating more. Some suggestions that have been found helpful for the overweight child include:

- Don't eat around a child who is trying to avoid food.
- Let him serve himself. Don't offer him food.
- Do not offer or cook foods rich in calories, such as fried foods or desserts; cut down on dairy foods and other foods high in fat and cholesterol.
- Avoid mentioning dieting, weight, or food restriction around your child.
- Don't compare him disparagingly with thin people.
- Don't urge him to lose weight.
- Don't use food gifts (even healthful ones!) as a reward.
- Encourage exercise by exercising yourself. Better yet, let exercise involve "fun" activities, which can include back-

packing (even at a large park), bicycling, rowing or canoeing, swimming, walking, or playing such games as badminton, baseball, basketball, handball, or soccer.

■ Whatever activity you choose, be sure it is not beyond your child's skills or ability.

■ Praise your child for any effort directed at improving his eating habits.

■ If you are planning on losing some weight yourself, make it a family activity but follow these same suggestions for yourself, your spouse, and other family members.

Is it all right for a child to start the Eating For A's Program if he's overweight? Let's suppose your child is 10 years old and 20 pounds overweight. Should the program be used to help him lose weight? No. Eating For A's is not a weight-loss program but one that builds healthy eating habits for a lifetime.

It is our philosophy that much more will be gained if your child learns to use food to *maintain* his weight, rather than to lose it by restricting his intake. If he becomes aware of which foods are best for his health, fitness, and academic performance, he will eventually stop gaining weight so fast. Instead, he will grow into his extra weight as he gets older, until he is within the desired range for his age, bone structure, and height. The key lies in helping your child *maintain* his weight because, if he is 20 pounds overweight at age 10, he will be within the desired weight range by age 12, without ever having to go on a weight-reducing program. After that, he will know how to eat at a level compatible with his energy output.

Severe calorie restriction for significant weight loss may be harmful to your child's health and interfere with his growth. We strongly discourage appetite-suppressing medications, unless recommended by your child's pediatrician. Most individuals who go on such medications usually gain the weight back after discontinuing it, and, because they rely on pills, do not learn how to eat properly or exercise to maintain their health and weight over a lifetime.

Eating Disorders

Some children develop bizarre eating habits very early in their lives, even before adolescence. Two serious eating disorders that warrant any parent's concern are *bulimia* and *anorexia nervosa*. In each condition, the child is so obsessed with the consumption of food and its effect on his body weight that he goes to extremes to control it. In both conditions there is a genuine fear of getting fat; simple reassurance that it won't happen provides no comfort.

BULIMIA

In bulimia, the individual has recurrent episodes of binge eating in which rapid consumption of large amounts of food occur over a short period of time. Patients with bulimia have reported that they can consume between 3,000 and 20,000 calories a *day*, yet gain little or no weight. They accomplish this by purging (vomiting) the food after each binge.

Some bulimics also resort to using laxatives or diuretic drugs with or without vomiting to get rid of their food. Studies have shown that each binge episode involves taking in an average of 1,200 calories. Such behavior, referred to as the "binge-purge syndrome," may begin in children as young as 10 or 11 and continue for many years, unnoticed by the family, schoolmates, or friends. It is much more common in females than males, although some school-age male athletes who practice sports where weight is important also use bulimia as a weight-control method.

Bulimia is a highly secretive activity which can go on for

many years before treatment is sought. If unchecked, it can lead to many medical complications. Also, if the bulimic vomits frequently, the stomach acids may remove the protective enamel on the teeth, leading to rampant dental decay. If you suspect bulimia, contact your physician immediately as there are many nutritional and behavioral treatment programs available. Many bulimics can be helped if given proper professional care by an eating disorder specialist.

ANOREXIA NERVOSA

Anorexia nervosa is a much more serious eating disorder in which the person restricts the intake of calories until he is gravely underweight. The mortality rate for anorexia nervosa is very high compared to other mental disorders. It may begin in children as young as 8 or 9, and persist for many years. Unlike the bulimic, the anorectic's obvious condition is very distressing for others. Many parents of anorectics implore their children to eat, only to find the child cannot "see" the problem. Even when placed in front of a mirror, these children have totally distorted images of their bodies and see themselves as fat.

This cognitive impairment is unique to this disorder and is one reason why treatment is so difficult. The disease is also serious because such restrictive dietary practices may lead to impairment of normal development, leading to potential heart failure, osteoporosis, and other related complications. If your child seems unusually thin and often refuses to eat, or eats too little, consider asking your physician for a complete examination. If he suspects anorexia nervosa, you can have an eating disorder specialist confirm the diagnosis.

Until recently, the treatment of anorexia nervosa and bulimia was very costly and brought poor long-term results. But in 1983, researchers studying patients with these two disorders discovered that many suffered from a zinc deficiency that could easily be diagnosed using a new zinc taste-test. In the past, zinc deficiency was not suspected because such diagnostic tests were not always reliable. With this new noninvasive and rapid technique, these patients can be tested quickly and inexpensively. It was not until 1990, however, that long-term clinical trials were reported, so the information is fairly new.

Stress seems to be a particular factor causing the loss of zinc in these patients. If they are found to be deficient, they can be treated with a new type of liquid zinc supplement for several days or weeks. Do not attempt to do this yourself— seek professional advice. Find a doctor who is familiar with the new protocol. Long-term studies have shown that this treatment, when combined with psychotherapy or other behavioral therapies and nutrition education, can bring eating disorders under control. You will find references for your doctor to read in the References section. If the doctor wants to use liquid zinc treatment the manufacturers will provide him with copies of the studies and brand names of liquid zinc: Zinc Status from Ethical Nutrients, Inc. and Zinc Talley from Metagenics, Inc., San Clemente, California.

OTHER MEDICAL DISORDERS

Should your child have special medical problems, such as diabetes, please consult your family physician or pediatrician before beginning our program. Children with recurrent diarrhea or with metabolic disorders warranting medication or careful attention to their diet need personalized attention and education that can only be given by trained nutritionists under the supervision of a physician.

4

GETTING READY

According to the late famous child psychologist Bruno Bettelheim, *"How one is being fed, and how one eats, has a larger impact on the personality than any other human experience . . . Eating experiences condition our entire attitude to the world, not so much because of how nutritious the food we are given is, but with what feelings and attitudes it is given. Around eating, for example, attitudes are learned or not learned, which are the preconditions for all academic achievement, such as the ability to control oneself . . . for future rewards."*

Enrolling Your Child in the Program

The most difficult task you will have is not getting rid of nonnutritious foods, not restocking your kitchen, not going shopping, and not even preparing new dishes. It is overcoming your child's resistance. This is true of all change, but is nowhere more evident than with food. The first step in overcoming resistance is to deal with it *before* it begins. And the way you do this is by enrolling your child's cooperation from the beginning.

He ought to feel that his help is welcome and essential. It has been our experience that enrolling your child at the very outset will facilitate making it *his* program. And this sense of ownership will greatly enhance its eventual success. In this way, the child will be sharing the responsibility for the program's success. If, from the very beginning, the child feels this is a *joint effort,* and that you are eating the same way he is, he will not feel that he is being singled out, or forced. But it is you, the parent, who must first take responsibility. You have already done this, in part, by purchasing this book. Now you must examine your attitudes.

PROVIDING A ROLE MODEL

Your own attitude toward food is as important as your child's. This is especially true because children learn by imitation. This puts your commitment to the program on the line. It will not work if you have a double standard—telling him he can no longer drink sodas, while you drink a Coke in front of him. (Incidentally, your own health and well-being will benefit from this.)

When you are a model for *young* children, be aware that they are particularly sensitive to your attitude, as indicated by gestures, facial expressions, and *how* you say something rather than *what* you say. For example, if you're eating cauliflower and you grimace while you're saying: "Mmmm-mmm—Try this! It's the best I've ever eaten," your grimace will be worth a thousand words. In short, if you're faking it, you better make sure you're doing so with your whole body.

BEHAVIORAL CONTRACTING

Most of our behavior is based on contracts, whether it is called that or not. Husbands and wives enter into agreements, more often verbal than written. A contract is a way of getting something from acting a certain way or doing a certain thing. If you want your child to eat certain foods, you have to enter into a contract with him. Contracting is a way to motivate him to change; he gets something for his cooperation.

For example: Billy is a 7-year-old who dislikes any green vegetables. But he admires his father and loves hearing stories about his childhood. Billy's father used contracting in the following way.

FATHER
Did I ever tell you the story of how I won the 100-yard dash in high school? It was a very close race.

BILLY
No, you didn't.

FATHER
Coming toward the finish line, we were all bunched together—like the peas on your plate. What's happening with those peas, anyway?

BILLY
I don't like them.

FATHER
I like them. And maybe you'll learn to. So anyway, we're approaching the finish line, and—are you going to finish them?

BILLY
No.

FATHER
Okay, three bites. We'll start together. Both of us. On the count of three. But you have to count *strong*—as strong as the peas will make you.

BILLY
Okay, I'm ready. One, two, three.

As Billy ate *his* peas, his father finished the story, and both were satisfied. The contract worked.

Naturally, the contract and its rewards will depend on the specific child's interests. But one point which applies to everyone is that food is *never* a reward. In other words, you never say, "If you eat your peas, you can have Jell-O for dessert." You never compensate good nutritious foods with minimally nutritious rewards.

It is essential that the child perceives the program as an act of love and caring on your part, and not as anything punitive or depriving. Even though he may act to the contrary, a child intrinsically feels you care when you set limits. Your love and caring form the motivation for taking on this program. You must convey this to your child. How you do this depends upon your relationship with him. No one knows him better than you; if anyone can motivate him at this stage, it will be you.

POSITIVE ASSOCIATIONS

Of course, a child will *fight* to eat the way he pleases—and one of the weapons you can use to disarm him is positive association. If you can find something *personal* that he likes, and make an association with a food, the food then becomes more appetizing. For instance, your son likes Ninja Turtles. You're serving him a green vegetable soup. Before he can say a word, you announce this as "Ninja Turtle Soup," a soup which will give him all the qualities of the Ninja Turtles, winning against impossible odds.

Or, for an older child, here's a true story we read. A mother made moussaka for dinner, a new dish that her children had never had before. Her oldest and youngest children seemed to enjoy it, but the middle son would not even taste it. His mother knew he was interested in Greek mythology, so she painted a verbal picture of Greek farmers raising eggplant and tending sheep by the blue Aegean two thousand years ago, and suggested that they may have stopped their work to discuss the gods and eat this very dish under the shade of a twisted olive tree. Her son tried the dish, and it has been one of his favorites ever since.

By themselves eggplant and lamb certainly rank low among children as food preferences. The only reasonable explanation for the child's willingness to try it was the pleasurable associations the dish was given by his mother's story.

THE DINING ENVIRONMENT

Pleasurable associations should begin with the dining environment. When you think of the most memorable meals you've had, you no doubt remember the atmosphere of the place, the friendly conversation, and the people around you as much as the food. *The same thing applies to your child.* If you are truly interested in changing his attitude about food, you will want to go out of your way to make his surroundings as pleasant as possible. This doesn't just mean the table setting, but also the lightness of the conversation and the positive attention being paid to him.

The opposite of this is a social situation fraught with tension and arguments. Unfortunately, many people remember their dinners at home with horror, and this association lingers in terms of their food habits. Dinnertime is really

EATING ENVIRONMENT

> In a study of American preschool children, companionship at meals, a positive home atmosphere, and appropriate food-related parenting behaviors were all found to be related to improvements in the quality of the diet.
>
> Does your home provide this kind of supportive, nurturing environment?

the only time a family has an opportunity to sit down together. It can become a time when the atmosphere is charged with all the problems that have been accumulating during the day.

It's important to talk about problems that concern the family *with the family*—but it's also important to find the *right time and place* to do it. And the dinner table is the wrong place. It's not good for digestion or for dealing with positive food changes. In fact, issues can probably better be dealt with in a forum specifically structured for that purpose: *after a pleasant dinner,* when people's hunger has been satisfied and they're feeling generally calm.

This is also another reason not to eat in front of the television. Dinner should be the one time when the family can experience itself—without interruptions or distractions. Watching television is also a way of "tuning out" from the meal, so that no attention is paid to the food nor is it given any significance. If a special program is scheduled which everyone wants to watch during dinnertime, then that can be used as a "treat"—another way for the family to do something "special" together.

WHAT YOU CAN DO WHEN CHILDREN REFUSE FOOD

Everyone—children in particular—dislike or think they dislike some foods even though they've never tried them. It is most important to overcome this because trying a food is the first step toward acceptance and liking. The opinions of others come in handy at this stage. If you can get your child's friend or a favored sibling to try the food and like it, then he may begin to believe that the food has some good qualities. Later on, he may even get to like it!

The old standby: "Take at least three bites" often works. You can decide the number of bites, and may even assign enough to have the whole dish finished!

If the food clearly doesn't taste good to a child, it really won't matter how anyone else feels about it, or what tactics you use.

But when a food is "important," you're going to have to work harder at getting him to eat it. Naturally, making it *taste good* is the key. One mother we know changes the way a food is prepared but *keeps on serving it again and again*, regardless of negative responses. As a last resort, she finally says, "You must eat it."

This worked beautifully with broccoli. For a long time, she served her son broccoli in many forms and he would continually call it "yuck." In the beginning, to get him started, she would allow some catsup and a little salt, but she would never give up. Finally, he had to eat it because she demanded that he do so. Eventually he developed a preference for it, and now says, "My favorite food is broccoli with brown rice." If you accept that a child doesn't like a food and act on that acceptance, then you're lost.

Stanley's Story: The Turning Point

Stanley was an inveterate candy-bar eater. He consumed Clark Bars, Hershey Bars, Reese's Pieces every day. His parents were somewhat nutritionally aware, but every time they tried to change his candy-bar habit, they would have terrible fights so they finally gave in. The rule in the house was that he come home from school and do homework before being allowed to play. Stanley had most of his candy on the way home from school so when his mother would lay out some healthful snacks, he wouldn't eat them because he said he wasn't hungry. The end result was that he never could concentrate on his homework. Instead, he watched television, which made him even more lethargic. Eventually, his grades suffered.

His parents realized that they would have to confront him, regardless of the fights. They told him that because they loved him, they were concerned about his future, and the seeds of his adult life were being planted right now in the sixth grade. They told him how proud they were of him—how bright he was, and how together they could work out a plan for him to take better care of himself. The candy bars would have to be replaced but there were other delicious things he could eat instead—fruit-juice sweetened cookies, sugarless candy, etc.

Naturally, he balked. For months afterward, his parents would find secret stashes of candy bars in his room. They generally ignored the stashes and continued to encourage him. The arguments went on, but one day after being sent to the store for some last-minute dinner items, Stanley brought back a healthful new dessert—unsweetened fruit ices. "This is something I bought for you to eat," he announced. His parents asked if he would join them and he said no, he wouldn't touch that stuff. They let it go until after the meal when his mother served three plates of the fruit ices—and without saying a word, Stanley ate his portion.

From that point on, Stanley began eating a little more sensibly. Clearly, he had finally acknowledged that his parents' actions were motivated by love and concern. Will Stanley still have a Mars Bar? Of course he will. But his awareness is now at a higher level, and once having crossed that threshold, there is no turning back. There's a good chance, if his parents keep reinforcing the positive results of nutritious eating, that he will eventually request more healthful snacks. In this sense, they will have succeeded in raising Stanley's consciousness.

Raising Your Child's Consciousness

A lot of people feel that it's not worth the trouble to fight with your child to change his eating pattern. They cite the fact that eating should be an *enjoyable* experience, and if you're constantly pressing a child to try foods he doesn't want, you're going to make the forbidden foods more attractive.

The Eating For A's Program is really aimed at a different goal. Ultimately, you are working to raise your child's consciousness about food, which will affect not only his childhood but the rest of his life. The efforts you make, and the fights you have in the beginning, are worth it because *it can be done.* We sometimes forget that if adults can have their consciousness raised, it is even easier to do with children because, despite the powerful effects of the anti-nutritional messages on television, they haven't built up decades of food prejudices.

In fact, although in some ways it's never been more difficult to instill good nutritional habits due to mass media advertising, it's also never been easier. This is because never before have such a variety of healthful foods and snacks been available. True, on the surface, many of them look more expensive, but if you analyze their nutritional content, they are not. You have to look at the tradeoff: it is cost-effective to spend more money on nutritious food than to save money on junk. We are not just talking about money—we're talking about your child's future and the quality of his life, now and in years to come.

HOW TO TALK ABOUT THE PROGRAM

One of the common mistakes parents make regarding good food is telling the whole truth. Nothing turns a child off faster than to be told to eat something "because it's good for you." He equates this with its not tasting good.

For instance, if you tell him that the reason you are starting this program is so that he has an opportunity to feel better, have more energy, and do better in school, you're likely to get nowhere fast. After all, children have no concept of the way they feel—except when they're sick. Probably, overall, he feels fine and has boundless energy. If he is able to evaluate how he performs in school, he makes no connection between his performance and his diet. Therefore, you will not motivate or encourage him by stressing that the food is good for him. Strike this expression from your vocabulary!

Also, if you start talking about the "learning nutrients," or the foods that contain them (particularly "yucky" foods like wheat germ and brewer's yeast) and how he'll be glad he followed the Eating For A's Program when he's older, you'll be wasting your breath. He just doesn't care about those ideas now.

So how do you proceed? You have to tell your child something about the program before you start because he will find out anyway. He'll be seeing you making your preparations and know something's going on, and he will feel left out if you don't tell him.

The feeling of being "left out" is something that you can

capitalize on. No child wants to be excluded, especially from his own family, and so you might have the following scenario:

MOTHER
We're going to start an exciting new eating program that everyone in the family is involved in. And we're going to have a lot of fun doing it. Do you want to have some fun?

CHILD
What is it?

MOTHER
Well, basically it's about eating in ways to make us smarter. It's going to give us more energy also.

CHILD
It sounds like I'm going to have to eat vegetables.

MOTHER
Maybe. If we're all eating vegetables.

CHILD
Vegetables aren't fun.

MOTHER
How do you know? We're not even eating, and you're already deciding. You don't want to be sitting with an empty plate, do you?

CHILD
Maybe.

MOTHER
No you don't, because then you'd be hungry all the time. And then you'll lose so much weight you'll become invisible. And then no one would see you, and they might accidentally sit on you, and then you'd be not only hungry but squashed.

No matter what the age of the child, a sense of humor is essential. There's a good chance, in the beginning, that the child will want to keep his "old" eating pattern as a way of holding on to his individuality. And that's where *choice* comes in. If a child is given choices (without compromising the program) then he will not feel something is being taken away from him. He will also feel good about himself because *he* has chosen the "right" food, and he will have a sense of independence.

However, there will be times when, no matter how clever you are, your child will not cooperate. You will have to insist and he will be angry. All you can do is to acknowledge the anger, permit him to have it, be loving, and stick to your guns.

Here's an example. The scene is a restaurant. Eleven-year-old Janet is about to have lunch with her mother. They are on the program and her mother has learned not to say maybe when forbidden foods are suggested because this is not a negotiable item.

JANET
If I eat everything, can I have an ice cream soda?

MOTHER
No, Janet. You know that you're not supposed to have them.

JANET
Why? Everybody has ice cream sodas for dessert. All my friends have them. Why can't I have it just this once?

MOTHER
You know we've agreed that there are certain foods we're not going to eat anymore. The ice cream sodas they serve here is one of them. Now let's talk about what you can have. You have a choice between melon, strawberries, fruit salad, yogurt, or we can make an ice cream soda when we get home."

At this point, Janet might have a tantrum. And the mother can say sympathetically, "I know this is difficult, and I know you're angry, and I'm not picking on you, but we must stick by our agreement. This doesn't mean you won't get what you want—you will, but you'll have to wait till we get home."

Throughout this book, in addition to recipes for healthful versions of some of the foods your child craves (like a soda recipe, p. 105), we will be giving you tips on how to have fun, play games, etc., to help motivate your child to eat better. At some point, you will no longer have to do this because your child will be aware of how much better he is feeling and performing.

THE FOOD DIARY

The first fun activity starts with a food diary that the child keeps himself. This is an excellent way to make him (and you) aware of exactly what his eating pattern is. For one thing, it will indicate how often the child snacks, and what kind of snacks he eats. It will also highlight food preferences and dislikes. A food diary should be kept for 3 to 5 days before beginning the program. It will be an excellent barometer of just how successful this program is in changing habits later on. It helps if everyone in the family keeps a diary and compares it with one another. This is part of the game; after all, you don't always eat together and this is a way of sharing and comparing what *everyone* eats at any time. The most important aspect of this is that the child does not feel singled out—but rather part of a cooperative plan.

You may have to do a young child's diary for him—he can illustrate it with pictures of food. Do not make it seem like homework or some sort of drudgery. The following is an example of a food diary. You can make copies and use it as is, or create your own. Be as original as you like and get your

FOOD DIARY

Think for a few minutes. What did you eat today? Try to remember. Then write down *everything* you can remember *eating* or *drinking* (no "forgetting" or cheating!)

MORNING:

Breakfast:_____

_____

Snacks: (Include drinks, gum, candy, etc.) _____

_____

AFTERNOON:

Lunch: _____

_____

Snacks: _____

_____

EVENING:

Dinner/Supper:_____

_____

Snacks: _____

What did you like best? _____

What did you like least? _____

child's input. Do all you can to keep your child involved in this essential activity.

GETTING OTHERS INTO THE ACT

Enrolling your child will be a great deal easier and more fun if you involve another family in the program. No doubt you have friends or neighbors who have similar issues with their children and who would be interested in making these changes. Try to arrange for them to start the program at the same time you do. The support you will give to one another will be immeasurable.

The Fourth Meal

When we were growing up, even if it was only twenty years ago, mealtimes seemed to be more structured. The norm was to have three meals a day, with an emphasis on a hearty dinner. Everyone ate the same thing at the same time. Nowadays, something different is happening. Children don't live in the same time frame as we did. If the world has speeded up for us parents, it is going even faster for children. And this is especially reflected in their eating habits.

If you were going to guess which meal provides the most energy for your child, what would it be? A good breakfast? A nutritious lunch? A hearty dinner? Snacks?

The answer, surprisingly, is snacks. According to the latest surveys, snacks now provide more energy than any single meal, and account for 30 percent of a child's daily caloric intake. In fact, snacks constitute the fourth meal of the day. The fourth meal is a new American eating phenomenon. And it's much more important than we realize.

One of the foundations of the Eating For A's Program is the

recognition that snacks can be as important as meals, that they can, in fact, substitute for meals, provided they are the right kind of snacks.

Most snacks that kids eat are high in fat, salt, sugar, and cholesterol. They lack not only nutritional value, but they throw off a child's chemistry and fill him with empty calories. He feels "well fed" but has no room in his stomach for other foods containing the important "learning nutrients." And, as we have said, most of the snack items that appeal to children are loaded with artificial colors and flavorings in amounts that can become dangerous for a child.

Each week the Eating For A's Program will introduce new alternative snacks to substitute for the nonnutritious ones. In this way, you will be nourishing your child with snacks as well as with meals.

SNACKS FOR DINNER?

From earliest childhood, children are snackers. The trick now is to learn how to incorporate this basic behavior into their daily eating pattern so that they can get the maximum nutrition. This means you will probably have to start rethinking what constitutes a meal—particularly dinner. In other words, if your child doesn't want what you've prepared for dinner, you have several solutions. You can try to force him, you can wait a few minutes and put it away and not give him anything else, you can try to coax, negotiate, play a game—or you can substitute.

If you choose to substitute, that may be the best decision. And the best substitution is—you guessed it—a snack.

In other words, snacks now take a greater importance than ever before. They not only constitute the fourth meal of the day but can actually become part of the other three. How? By careful planning, being one step ahead of your child, you can prepare snacks and have them ready to substitute for whole meals.

Will healthful snacks provide a meal's worth of nutrition? Yes. Once you establish the pattern of eating healthful snacks and eliminate the unhealthy ones, you will have accomplished one of the major goals of the Eating For A's Program. Why? Because, whether inside or outside the home, a child is more likely to counteract the value of the learning nutrients he has eaten if he snacks improperly.

In Chapter 6, you'll be starting your new snacks program. The way in which you organize your kitchen will be a great help to you in this regard, so now it's time to look at your kitchen.

5

THE EATING FOR A'S KITCHEN

The Eating For A's kitchen is a natural foods kitchen and is built around the principle of having the foods rich in learning nutrients easily available for the whole family. To do this, we're going to examine (1) the food in your pantry, refrigerator, and freezer and (2) your kitchen equipment.

Assessing Your Kitchen

Assessing your kitchen is relatively easy and can in fact be enjoyable (it's sometimes good for the soul to take stock). It involves looking at what you have with a new awareness, but it does not mean making any drastic changes. As with everything else in this book, you should go slow at first.

DISCARDING AND REPLACING

At the beginning of each week, Eating For A's provides a list of items to be discarded, and a list of replacement items for which you will shop. In this way, you will be making the transition painlessly. By the end of the program, the items in your pantry, refrigerator, and freezer will bear little resemblance to what's there now.

GOOD, BETTER, BEST

Discarding and replacing foods can be facilitated by what we call the "good, better, best" approach. Here's how it works. Let's take bread as an example. Many commercial breads contain ingredients that are far from natural: emulsifiers, dough conditioners, preservatives, artificial colorings, and a variety of sweeteners such as white sugar, caramel coloring, corn syrup, etc.

Bread in the "good" category would not have any of the ingredients listed above. In addition, if it's white bread (and for now, it probably will be) it should be made with unbleached—not bleached—flour. Unbleached flour still does not contain the amount of fiber or the wheat germ and bran found in whole wheat flour, but it has not gone through the additional process of bleaching. In the first two weeks of the program, you will be making changes to include foods that fall into the "good" category. Then, you will proceed to "better," which is the next category. In addition to not containing any of the additives mentioned above, better bread would be whole wheat instead of white. In this way, you will be getting the grain in its natural state—with the wheat germ and bran intact.

Beware, when reading labels, of "wheat flour"—this does not mean whole wheat. Also some so-called whole wheat breads only look that way. They are actually made from white flour and are colored with caramel coloring. Read the labels carefully so you don't get fooled.

WHOLE WHEAT NUTRITIONAL ADVANTAGES
WHOLE WHEAT VS. WHITE ENRICHED FLOUR

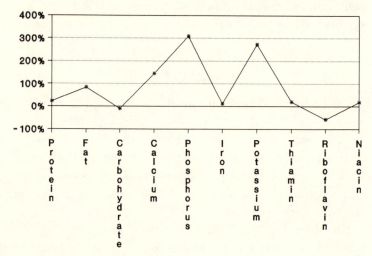

Source: USDA Handbook No. 466 (1975)

Toward the end of the 12 weeks, you will begin introducing food in the "best" category. "Best" bread is made from organically grown wheat, not sweetened at all (or just sweetened with fruit juice). When we get to the "best" category, you will be able to find excellent items in natural food stores; or you may want to experiment with baking your own bread—an effort that is more than rewarded by both taste and the aroma that will fill the house. (See Suggested Reading for books containing delicious bread recipes.)

Realistically, most of us won't eat at this "best" level consistently, but it gives us something to aspire to and keeps our awareness keen.

You can see that with this step-by-step approach you are not only making the transition easier for yourself (in terms of buying and preparing) but you are also changing your child's

taste buds *slowly* so that the "best" food will be more acceptable when it is introduced.

EQUIPMENT

In all likelihood, you probably already have what you
need. However, working with natural foods is facilitated by a
few good (and always sharp) *knives for paring, cutting, or
chopping* vegetables. A *natural bristle vegetable brush* is
essential because you will want to keep peeling to a minimum
(many valuable nutrients are in, or just under, the skin of
vegetables and fruits). You should have a *blender* for its
versatility. Although a *food processor* is very convenient, if
you don't own one, many of its functions can be done by a
hand shredder, chopper, etc. For grinding seeds and nuts, you
could use an old-fashioned mortar and pestle, but a *small
electric grinder* (like those used for coffee) is far more efficient
and time-saving.

Cookware should be made of heavy-duty stainless steel
(with some reinforcement on the bottom for even cooking),
iron, or glass. Aluminum is generally unacceptable because
it leaches into foodstuffs (particularly acidic ones) and can be
harmful over a period of time. Enamel pots are impractical
because they can chip and then have to be discarded.

One of the most important helpers you can have is a
steamer. Steaming retains the vitamins and minerals in vegetables and allows you to keep them firm, not overcooked and
mushy. Many items can serve as steamers, but the best are
either a small collapsible stainless-steel basket, which folds
to adapt to most pans, or a set of bamboo steamers, which can
hold an entire meal and fit easily into a wok or any pan deep
enough to steam in. To accompany your pans, have a variety
of *wooden spoons and spatulas*—wood will not scratch pans
and is gentler for stirring or mixing food.

Using the following list, you can now assess your equipment. Check the items you already have and note those you will need to replace or purchase.

Checklist

- ☐ *knives*
- ☐ *vegetable brush*
- ☐ *blender*
- ☐ *food processor*
- ☐ *small electric grinder*
- ☐ *cookware*
- ☐ *steamer*
- ☐ *wooden spoons and spatulas*

Going Shopping for the Basics

The human body is finite and perhaps nothing in it is more finite than our stomachs. Stated simply, we can healthily fit *only* so much into our stomachs within the course of a day. No one knows this better than food manufacturers. So, in order to stay in business, they have to compete successfully with each other for your finite appetite. For example, let's say your children like cold cereal and eat it for breakfast almost every day. Maybe the family goes through a box of cereal a week—maybe two. But there are dozens of different kinds of cereal available in the supermarket from which to choose.

The only way to shop smartly is to realize that you have choices—and only you can ensure the healthful eating habits of your children by making the right choices, those based on some information and sharp scrutiny. You can pass this notion on to your children as well. They may not realize how easily their choices are influenced by:

- TV
- their peers
- the location of foods in the supermarket
- eye-catching "sexy" packaging
- premiums, like contests printed on boxes or prizes buried in them.

Enrolling your children in the 12-week program will be aided considerably by making them educated consumers. Take the older children with you on your first shopping trip so you can share this new experience together. (Conversely, it may not be wise to take young children—they're much too impressionable and the process of retraining their choices may have to be more gradual.) And, an additional word of caution: During the first weeks of the program, don't let anyone else take them shopping. Grandparents, in particular, are easy marks when it comes to a child's pleading for a treat in the store!

For your first shopping trip, the supermarket will suffice. These days, ordinary supermarkets carry many food items that were once only available in natural food stores. In subsequent weeks, you will probably need to do some shopping at a natural food store. When that time comes, we will guide you, suggesting you shop there for only those items that are impossible to get elsewhere. (The sad fact is that natural food stores are usually more expensive than supermarkets.)

The only other information you need for your first shopping trip is how to read a label. This isn't hard and the following tips should make you an expert.

A SHORT COURSE IN LABEL READING

1. Start with the *name of the product*. Some companies change the name, but don't be fooled into thinking the

product has been improved nutritionally. One example: Kellogg's changed Sugar Frosted Flakes to Frosted Flakes in 1983 (probably because sugared cereals were getting such bad press), but the ingredients remained the same. *So, even if you think you know about a product, you must read the label.*

Another point about the name: the words *quick* and *instant* are buzzwords; they invariably target foods that contain additives and are always more expensive.

2. *Weight:* All ingredients are listed in order of weight; the product contains the most of the first ingredient, and the least of the last.

3. *Legal deception:* The same thing often has different names. Food manufacturers are masters of "legal deception." The prime example are the names used to describe various sugars on food labels:

artificial sweeteners
aspartame
Barbados molasses
blackstrap molasses
buttered syrup
caramel
carob syrup
corn syrup
dextran
dextrose
diastase
diastatic malt
dried corn syrup

ethyl maltol
glucose
glucose solids
golden syrup
honey
maple syrup
molasses
nonnutritive sweeteners
refiner's syrup
saccharin
sorbitol
sucrose
turbinado sugar

As should the above, all the following should be approached with caution:

beet sugar	golden sugar	rare food sugars
brown sugar	grape sugar	raw sugar
cane sugar	invert sugar	yellow sugar
date sugar	invert sugar syrup	

You will find specifics on this throughout the book.

4. *Nutritional information,* such as amounts of protein, carbohydrate, etc., is listed for serving size. Carbohydrate and fat percentages may be misleading. Example: One candy bar says its carbohydrate content is "15 grams," but a more accurate description would be 44 percent sugar. Regarding fats, the percentages of saturated, polyunsaturated and mono-unsaturated fats should be listed. Often only the word *fat* appears so you have no way of knowing if it's the worst kind (saturated).

5. *Standardized labeling:* Some foods are not required to have ingredients listed on the label because the FDA has set up a "standard" for them. Examples of this are mayonnaise, catsup, and about 300 other foods. Catsup, in particular, by law can have up to 30 percent additional sugar without disclosing it on the label; in fact, only "imitation" catsup has no sugar. We strongly advise you to avoid any foods that do not list ingredients.

6. *Additives and preservatives:* This is a vast topic and we can only speak of it in the most generalized way. A rule of thumb is to avoid all artificial colorings and flavorings, *MSG* (monosodium glutamate), *BHA, BHT, propyl gallate, sodium nitrite, sodium nitrate, caffeine, sulfur dioxide, benzoic acid (benzoates), and sodium bisulfite.* By government regulation, some additives are listed as "artificial" even though the ingredients themselves are natural, because they are not natural to that particular food—for example, beet powder,

which is used to make food red. Use your judgment where these additives are concerned.

The best suggestion is to avoid all foods with long scientific (and often unpronounceable) names. Chances are that most of these additives come from a laboratory and are not natural.

7. *Fortification:* Most packaged and prepared foods are over-fortified, giving us more than we need and adding to the price of the product. More important, fortification is misleading. It makes us think something is good nutritionally when this may not be the case at all. Fortification will not turn an unhealthful food into a healthful one. A small amount of

LABEL READING

E ven if you are careful about reading labels, you had better become familiar with federal guidelines which allow sugar to be listed 11 different ways, using names of sugar compounds unfamiliar to us, hiding the fact that the food's main ingredient *is* actually sugar. Or if you're trying to reduce your fat or calorie intake, you better bring your calculator. Try to follow what we are about to explain. Say you are trying to buy a precooked dinner meal for your family. You look at the "low-calorie" claims on the label which tell you that there are "only" 25 grams of fat" in the box. Doesn't sound like much, does it? But think again. There are 9 *calories* in every gram of fat, so you have to multiply 25 times 9 to arrive at the figure of 225 calories. So, when you calculate the percentage of calories from fat in the entire box, you might discover that the meal is actually 60 percent fat! *No wonder it tastes so good!.* Why not have two or three boxes, it's low-calorie, isn't it?

Also beware of "cholesterol-free" labels. Cholesterol and fat are not the same. A food may contain no cholesterol but be loaded with saturated fat which raises cholesterol levels in the blood.

fortification may be all right (such as vitamind D in milk), but in general, don't be fooled by "fortified with . . ."

8. *Labeling:* If you wear reading glasses, make sure to take them to the supermarket. Some ingredient labeling is both hard to find and very small (deliberately?). Sometimes, you may feel you even need a microscope!

GENERAL SHOPPING TIPS

- **Concentrate on the outer aisles.** The areas around the edges of the supermarket are where the fresh produce and other more nutritious foods are found.
- **Beware of packages on the lower shelves** and at the checkout counter—these are designed to attract the "little people," young children who are influenced, usually by television, to be impulsive junk-food shoppers.
- **Be ready to switch brands.** Often different brands contain the same item, ingredient for ingredient, but there may be a wide spread in price. The same goes for packaging; fancy packaging seriously raises the price. Remember, you don't eat the box.
- **Bring (or buy) some celery or carrot sticks** or pieces of apple for your child to snack on while you're shopping. Nothing stimulates the tastebuds as much as seeing all that food lined up on the shelves, and you want to avoid an attack of "I'm hungry. Buy me that" while you are stocking up on good food.
- **Avoid purchasing items in large, bulk-size quantities.** Even though, eventually, this may prove to be a more time-saving and economical practice, until you have acquainted your child with some of these unfamiliar foods, it is better to start small. All fresh vegetables, fruits, meat, and fish should be bought for immediate

use whenever possible. Even with the best storage practices, essential vitamin and mineral losses take place.

Storage

You will probably be purchasing some unfamiliar food items and may be unsure about where to store them. Refer to the following list:

Nonfat dry milk powder	Cool (under 68 degrees), airtight container.
Wheat germ	Refrigerator, airtight container.
Bread (without preservatives)	Refrigerator, well-wrapped.
Oils (without preservatives)	Refrigerator.
Dried fruits	Cool (under 68 degrees), airtight container; avoid storing in plastic bags.
Nuts (shelled)	Room temperature, tightly closed glass container, if using within a few days. For longer time, store in refrigerator.
Nuts (unshelled)	Room temperature or under 68 degrees.
Nut butters	Cool, before opening. Refrigerator, once opened. Store upside down to help mix surface oil.
Honey	Room temperature; heat gently or place jar in warm water to soften or break up crystals.
Brewer's yeast	Refrigerator, once opened.

| Vegetables (fresh greens) | Refrigerator, best stored open or in brown paper bags, if using quickly. If storing in plastic, use paper towels or sponges to absorb excess water. |
| Tomatoes, white potatoes, avocados | Store at room temperature. |

After you get into the *natural food habit*, you may find you must shift where you store your groceries. Because one of the things that defines natural foods is the lack of preservatives, they do best when refrigerated and sometimes (if you're buying in bulk) frozen. For instance, whole grains such as brown rice or wheat berries contain essential oils which could go rancid if left at room temperature. On the other hand, visibility and accessibility can lead to better eating patterns. For this reason, nuts and seeds (in quantities that can be eaten quickly) should be stored in glass containers and prominently displayed.

Ideally, a cook using natural foods should have a lot of refrigerator space, but you can manage even with a small refrigerator if you purchase smaller quantities of certain items.

How to Introduce New Foods

You are now ready to begin your child's new eating program. But before you go into the kitchen, it is necessary to understand one of Eating For A's principles. In fact, this may be one of the most important sections you read in this book.

Even though you have begun enrolling your child in his new eating program, it would be a mistake to tell him exactly how you're going to do it. Parents are always being cautioned not to deceive their children. It's excellent advice—except that it has to be tempered with practical common sense.

THE "SNEAKY" COOK

In other words, at the onset of this program, certain food items must be "sneaked" in. The reason for this is simple: Most people (adults included) are skittish about trying new, unfamiliar foods. That is, if they *know*. But you have the chance to introduce many important learning nutrients without anyone knowing. Such items as *brewer's yeast, wheat germ, and dry milk powder are natural fortifiers* (as opposed to the chemical fortifiers found in many foods). They can be added to regular dishes without being detected. The recipes in the following chapters will explain how. Chances are that if you told your child that his favorite meat loaf contained some wheat germ, he would immediately reject it without so much as one taste. So why tell him? We promise that he'll never know because the recipes in this book have been child-tested for taste and appearance.

Will you have to be a sneak forever? Of course not. As the program progresses, and the results become apparent, your child's taste in foods will also change. At some point, everything will be out in the open and you will be able to discuss freely exactly what went into the food. The irony is that by that time everyone will probably have caught on anyway.

Food Preparation Tips

There is no question that preparing the food for the Eating For A's Program is somewhat more labor-intensive than what you may be used to. These are hectic times and most of us no longer spend even half the time our parents did in the kitchen. The tips below and throughout the book demonstrate our attention to this concern. But the era of "fast food"— whether it be at McDonald's or in the kitchen—is what got us into this mess to begin with. Therefore, you may have to put in a bit more time and effort, but be assured that the tradeoff in terms of your child's health and achievement will be more than worth it.

TIME-SAVING TIPS FOR SHOPPING

- Keep a reasonable supply of staples such as spices, dry goods, eggs on hand.
- Buy food in quantities close to what is required by the recipes you are using.
- Even though you may lose some of the vitamins, wash, thoroughly dry, and chop vegetables and fruit right after unpacking them. Store in plastic bags with a sponge or paper towel to absorb moisture.

TIME-SAVING TIPS FOR MEAL PREPARATION

- Hot water boils faster; for small amounts use the microwave.
- Measure "like ingredients" together (dry with dry; liquid with liquid) in a large measuring cup to avoid using a mixing bowl.
- Small items cook faster; buy small potatoes, etc., and serve more if necessary.
- Get your child into the habit of helping you prepare meals. This involvement may also foster more enthusiasm for the finished dish.

■ For bag lunches, use leftovers either in sandwiches or wrapped "as is." Prepare lunches the night before and add items like lettuce or tomatoes to sandwiches in the morning. For a change of pace, pack sandwich items in containers or plastic wrap and have your child assemble them at lunchtime. Sandwiches can be frozen in quantity: simply spread butter or good margarine to cover an entire bread slice, then add the filling, cover tightly, and freeze. Frozen sandwiches will defrost at room temperature in two or three hours.

NOTE: Items that do not freeze well are mayonnaise, raw vegetables or fruit, cooked egg whites, and natural cheese.

GENERAL TIPS ON MENU PLANNING

Plan ahead: This program is based on careful menu planning, not on spur of the moment. Planning ahead will save time, money, and, most important, will help you avoid making the wrong food choices.

Think about aesthetics: We all eat "with our eyes," so make meals colorful and varied. Your child's palate will respond to the palette of colors on the plate. Nothing is a greater turnoff than a monochromatic meal (white potatoes, white fish, white cauliflower). Also, vary the textures. A dish full of only crunchy foods is a bore (and also hard on the jaws). Similarly, while smooth food may work for someone in a sick bed it is hardly appealing to a healthy child.

Pay attention to portion sizes: When introducing any new food, start small. You can always give seconds if it's a big hit, but it's overwhelming for a child to face a pile of something unfamiliar, particularly if he has a small appetite to begin with.

Timing is essential: A meal should take a reasonable amount of time. Although you want to give your child every chance to eat his food, don't overdo it. When you introduce something new and it is not eaten within a half hour (at the most), take it away. Do not have a discussion about it. If you want to offer a snack substitution, you can do so at this point. Otherwise, simply remove the plate.

6

THE PROGRAM BEGINS

Looking at the Whole Program

Even though the Eating For A's Program progresses from nonnutritious to optimally nutritious food, there is valuable information in each week that should be used. For instance, the discussion of vegetables in Week Two is not exclusive to Week Two but is also valid for all the successive weeks and should be referred to as often as necessary. The weeks are set up this way because this is not a typical diet program. In a typical diet program, you are taken step by step, day by day, meal by meal. To do the Eating For A's Program this way would. be too limiting. Instead, you are asked to look at the program in its entirety. For this reason, it is important that you read through *all the weeks* before beginning Week One.

Choices

In Chapter 4 we stressed the need for children to have food choices, and it's just as important for *you* to have a choice.

For instance, if we said on Monday that you give your child orange juice or tomato juice, and you know that your child doesn't like either, you might be stuck without an alternative. By listing *all* the juice possibilities, and the references to the nutrients they contain, you have a free range of choice.

In regard to choice, it should be noted that the single most important factor in the success of the New York City school food program was the *choices offered the children*. Similarly, you will be able to offer your own child a variety of choices by not being locked into menu items for each day. In this way, the Eating For A's Program is giving you *tools* which will go beyond the 12 weeks and help you formulate a maintenance program for as long as you're feeding your child.

Ingredient Substitutions in Recipes

The menus and recipes for the 12 weeks of the program are presented to make it as easy and enjoyable for you as possible. It would be unrealistic to have you discard all your standard recipes and start from scratch. It is also unnecessary. Think of the menu suggestions and sample recipes as a road map for change. By understanding the guidelines and the goals of each week, it will be possible for you to adapt your own and others' recipes, as well as including ours. For instance, you may have a favorite recipe that has a certain ingredient, such as sugar, you will no longer be using. To help you change the recipe, we have provided in Chapter 7 (Week Eight, pp. 185–88) a list that shows you how and in what quantities to substitute more nutritious ingredients for standard ones.

VITAMIN/MINERAL SUPPLEMENTS

Most professional medical and dietetic associations have published policy statements saying that vitamin/mineral supplements are *not* recommended for *healthy* adolescents or children consuming an adequate well-balanced diet. However, many parents are incapable of determining if their child's diet is adequate and well balanced, or if it provides sufficient quantities of all the "learning nutrients." For this reason, we have no objection to parents selecting a *high-quality pediatric supplement* in the early part of the program—the first eight weeks. By the third month, however, your child will be getting more than enough of all the "learning nutrients" and other essential nutrients from the foods you serve.

Be sure you have information on the supplement's digestibility from a reliable source—it is important that these supplements break down in the stomach within a half hour after ingestion in order to ensure your child gets the value of the vitamins and minerals.

WEEK ONE

GOALS FOR THIS WEEK

- Concentrating on more nutritious breakfasts
- Reducing refined sugar
- Cutting down non-nutritious snacks and sodas
- Introducing some new snack items

SHOPPING LIST

Ingredients for Athlete's Mix (see p. 95)

"Good" whole wheat bread (no preservatives, sugar, corn syrup, caramel coloring)

"Healthier" sodas sweetened with fructose only, containing no caffeine, no artificial colors or flavors, no artificial sweeteners, such as NutraSweet [aspartame], saccharin, etc. One good brand is Best Health.

Unsweetened fruit juice (can still be made from concentrate). Beware of "fruit drinks" or punches; they usually contain only 10 percent fruit juice; the rest is water, sugar, and artificial flavors. Brands such as Hawaiian Punch, Hi-C, Kool-Aid, etc., are definitely not allowed!

Rice or corn cakes

Toasted wheat germ

"Good" hot cereals: Quaker Oats (can be quick-cooking), Wheatena, Mother's Oat Bran

"Good" cold cereals: Special K, Total, Shredded Wheat, Familia, Puffed Wheat, Puffed Rice

Peanut butter without sugar (nonhydrogenated, but can contain salt)

If you want to stock up on staples, you can buy the following items in the "good" category:

Bread (unbleached white flour, whole wheat without preservatives)

Oil (canola, virgin olive oil without preservatives)

Honey, maple syrup (pure, no added sugar)

Jams/preserves (low sugar or fruit juice-sweetened; no artificial colors or flavors)

Dried fruit (no added sugar; try to avoid preservatives such as sulfur dioxide)
Nuts, seeds (no added oil, sugar, or salt)
Crackers (unbleached white flour, rye, or whole wheat; no added sugar or preservatives)

ITEMS TO DISCARD

- All cereal with added sugar, artificial colors, and flavors (see list of sugars, pp. 78–79). Some major offenders are Apple Jacks (55 percent sugar), Froot Loops (53 percent sugar), Boo Berry (45 percent sugar), Lucky Charms (50 percent sugar)
- Other items with artificial flavors or colors
- All juice drinks and punches
- All fruits canned in heavy syrup

Menus—Week One

Include fruit; or fruit juice (whole fruit is preferable to fruit juice because of its fiber); cold or hot cereal or other grains (pancakes, etc.) or eggs; milk.

Fruit
Orange, fresh slices or wedges
Grapefruit, fresh halves or wedges; or canned without sugar or syrup
Fruit cocktail, fresh or jarred (no sugar or syrup)
Melon
Pineapple, fresh or canned (in water or juice only)
Stewed prunes, homemade or jarred (no sugar or syrup)
Dried Fruit Compote (see recipe, p. 98)

Juice
Orange
Grapefruit
Pineapple
Mixed fruit
Tomato
V-8
Grape
Apple
Apricot

Cereals
Acceptable cold cereals include:
  Shredded Wheat
  Grape Nuts
  Granola without added sugar (read labels carefully for
    hidden sugars and high fat content)
  Cold cereals (see p. 91)
  Hot cereals (see p. 141)

Eggs
Egg in a Circle (see recipe, p. 101) or any style eggs

Grains
Almost Wheat Cakes (see recipe, p. 100) or other pan-
  cakes
French Toast (see recipe, p. 100)
Whole wheat toast, apricot/orange jam (see recipe, p. 99)
  or jam with low or no sugar
Muffins (with reduced or no sugar)

O ne enlightened mother tells the story of how her 13-year-old son requested that the sandwiches be made with the white side up, so that no one would notice!)

LUNCH/DINNER

NOTE: If your child participates in the school breakfast and/or lunch program, chances are that he will not be getting meals that meet the standards of the Eating For A's Program. During the first few weeks, this is probably acceptable (providing the program is not horrendous). After that, you will probably have to provide a bag lunch that follows the Eating For A's guidelines. If it is necessary for your child to eat the school food, you may have to get involved in trying to make some substantive changes (which will also benefit many other children). For details on how to do this, see Chapter 11, Eating for A's Questions and Answers, pp. 243–45.

In Week One the emphasis is on breakfast. You do not have to make any changes in lunch or dinner. However, if possible, sandwiches should be made with one slice of white and one slice of whole wheat bread (see recipe for Ironed Sandwich, p. 99).

As for sandwich fillings, try to eliminate processed luncheon meats which contain large amounts of chemicals such as sodium nitrite, as well as artificial coloring and saturated fat.

A NOTE ABOUT DESSERTS

If you are accustomed to serving desserts, continue to do so during this week, but when at all possible omit those with added sugar (commercial cakes such as Hostess Twinkies, Devil Dogs, fruit pies, etc., are definitely not recommended). As the program progresses, there will be suggestions for dessert. The major problem in the beginning is that until your child can differentiate between a "good" and a "bad" dessert, there may be too much confusion. For example, if you serve a cake with all nutritious ingredients, it's still a cake so he may feel *any* cake is then acceptable. For this reason, we recommend things like fruit for dessert until later in the program.

New Snacks

ATHLETE'S MIX

The first new snack food on the Eating For A's Program is Athlete's Mix, and it's also the most popular Eating For A's snack. It is a mixture of natural, unsalted nuts, seeds, and dried fruits. If it is kept available on the counter, a child can add it to his cereal in the morning, take it with him for a lunch snack, eat it immediately when he comes home after school—even take it to the movies.

The most important point about the Eating For A's Program is to realize that when healthful snacks are around, children will begin to eat them. Therefore, before you even begin to set up your new kitchen, you should either make or buy Athlete's Mix. It's the ideal snack for kids because it's naturally sweet, contains many learning nutrients, and is both tasty and filling.

Here are the possible ingredients for Athlete's Mix:

Nuts: Almonds, cashews, Brazil nuts, peanuts, pecans, pine nuts (pignolia), walnuts
Seeds: Sunflower, pumpkin, sesame
NOTE: Nuts and seeds should be raw and unsalted, if your

child will accept them. If not, at this stage of the program they can be roasted and/or salted.

Dried Fruit: Apples, apricots, raisins, prunes, figs, cherries, banana chips (unsweetened), pineapple, papaya (unsweetened)

Miscellaneous: Roasted soybeans

These ingredients offer an excellent opportunity to involve your child in the program. Show him the list and let him pick the items he wants to include in this first batch of Athlete's Mix you make. Then, when you go shopping, either with or without him, these will be the items to buy.

You can also buy the equivalent of Athlete's Mix already packaged in natural food stores, but it will probably be less expensive if you make it yourself. Moreover, you will be sure of the ingredients (some dried fruits have added sugar), and you can select the items your child likes best. Remember that in the beginning he might not be keen on it, but our experience has proven that if Athlete's Mix is left around the kitchen constantly, and if he has participated in its preparation, a child will first nibble at it and then begin to eat it more regularly. Athlete's Mix is so important that we recommend you always have it on hand throughout this program.

One of the goals in this week is to begin reducing your child's consumption of refined sugar. If your child regularly snacks on sugary foods, you should set the following ground rule:

■ Only one item with sugar daily (this does not apply to soft drinks, which are discussed in Week Two). At this point, it can be anything he chooses, but it can only be *one*. He will still be able to snack as much as he likes on more healthful snacks.

In addition to Athlete's Mix, you can add the following snack items:

- Dried fruit (raisins, apricots, prunes, etc.): These may contain sulfur dioxide as a preservative. Remember, we're still at the crawling stage!
- Nuts: Almonds and cashews are preferable, but other nuts are acceptable. Nuts can be roasted and salted. Caution: Do not feed nuts to a child of two or under as they may choke on them.
- Whole-grain crackers, rice or corn cakes: At this point, you may still be spreading them with standard (sugared) jelly or jam and standard peanut butter.
- Popcorn (plain or with a small amount of butter and salt): It's easy to pop your own corn by buying the types that can just be heated on the stove or in the microwave. In this way, you can control the amount of butter and salt.
- Potato chips (unsalted)
- Pretzels (unsalted, preferably whole wheat)
- Cheese slices or chunks (low fat)
- Any fresh fruit

WEEK ONE

Recipes

DRIED FRUIT COMPOTE
SERVES: 3–4

> ½ *cup dried apricots*
> ½ *cup dried prunes*
> ½ *cup dried peaches*
> ¼ *cup raisins*
> ¼ *cup dried pears*
> 2 *tablespoons fresh lemon juice plus 1 teaspoon grated*
> *rind*
> 1 *orange, cut in thin slices*
> 2 *teaspoons cinnamon or 1 cinnamon stick*
> 2 *cups water*

1. Combine all ingredients in a saucepan and bring to a boil.

2. Lower heat, cover and simmer until fruit is cooked but not soft.

3. Allow to cool and serve; or refrigerate in covered container for later use.

NOTE: If fruit is soaked in advance, cooking time may be reduced.

Variations:

1. Substitute other dried fruits, but be sure to use apricots and raisins for nutrient value (see Nutrient Values List, p. 253).

2. Combine very ripe fresh fruit (a good way to use up bruised fruits) with dried fruit.

IRONED SANDWICH

YIELD: 1 SANDWICH

Older children will enjoy making this sandwich themselves.

> *1 slice unbleached white bread*
> *1 slice whole wheat bread*
> *Butter or margarine*
> *1 slice unprocessed yellow, muenster, or Swiss cheese*

1. Butter one side of each bread slice.
2. Place cheese between slices on unbuttered side.
3. Wrap sandwich in foil and iron until cheese melts.

Variation: You can dress up this sandwich with a slice of tomato, avocado, and/or alfalfa sprouts. It can be served for lunch or as a snack.

APRICOT/ORANGE JAM

YIELD: 1 CUP

> *8 ounces dried apricots*
> *½ pint water*
> *2 oranges*

1. Bring apricots and water to a boil, reduce heat and cook for 20 minutes or until tender.
2. Meanwhile, peel oranges, grate peel, and chop oranges fine.
3. Place apricots and water in food processor and process until smooth.
4. Add oranges and rind; mix well and store in refrigerator for up to two weeks.

NOTE: If smoother consistency is desired, process oranges and peel with apricots.

FRENCH TOAST
SERVES: 1

Since this is well browned, you can use whole wheat bread without detection.

> *1 egg, well beaten*
> *2 tablespoons low-fat milk, orange juice, water, or a*
> *   combination of each*
> *1 teaspoon vanilla extract*
> *1 slice whole wheat bread*
> *Canola oil or butter*

1. Combine egg, milk (or other liquid), and vanilla.
2. Place bread in mixture and let soak.
3. Heat pan or griddle, lightly grease with oil or butter. Fry bread until well browned on both sides. Serve with pure maple syrup, honey, or sugarless jam.

ALMOST WHEAT CAKES
SERVES: 4

> *1 cup whole wheat pastry flour*
> *1 cup unbleached white flour*
> *2 tablespoons toasted wheat germ*
> *2 teaspoons baking powder (non-aluminum may be*
> *   purchased in natural food store)*
> *2 cups nonfat milk (liquid or made from powder) or 1*
> *   cup nonfat milk and 1 cup plain nonfat yogurt*
> *1 egg, beaten*
> *1 tablespoon canola oil*
> *1 teaspoon vanilla extract*

1. Mix first four ingredients together.
2. Combine milk, egg, oil, and vanilla and blend well.

3. Stir lightly or put in blender (do not overmix; mixture should be slightly lumpy).

4. Lightly grease a pan or griddle with canola oil (or spray with El Molino canola mist, a healthful alternative to Pam). Heat well.

5. Drop mixture by spoonfuls and turn when surface bubbles and bottom side is brown.

6. Serve with pure maple syrup, honey, sugarless jam, fresh fruit mixed with plain nonfat yogurt or fruit-flavored yogurt (without sugar), apple butter, or unsweetened applesauce.

Variations: The following are variations which can be used in later weeks when your child is ready for more whole grains:

1. *For Multi-Grain Pancakes:* replace all white flour with whole grain flour such as whole wheat, buckwheat, soy, corn, or blue corn; you can experiment with combinations of these for taste and texture.

2. Replace whole milk with low-fat or nonfat milk, dry nonfat milk powder (best of all milks), yogurt, whole soy milk, or soy milk powder.

3. Use 1 tablespoon of ground or whole almonds, cashews, pumpkin or sunflower seeds as additional filler.

4. Add fresh fruit or berries or dried fruit (soaked slightly) to pancake batter as desired.

EGG IN THE CIRCLE

SERVES: 1

Children may enjoy making this themselves and will be even more eager to eat it.

> *1 slice whole wheat bread*
> *Butter or margarine*
> *1 egg*

1. Make a circle in the center of bread slice with a cookie cutter or rim of a glass and remove the circle; then butter both sides of the remaining bread slice.

2. Crack egg into a cup.

3. Heat a small frying pan and fry bread until it is browned on the bottom.

4. Carefully slip the egg over the circle; cover the pan until the white is set, then uncover and continue cooking until the egg is done (yolk will set in about 5 minutes).

Variation: Add a slice of cheese or some grated cheese after adding the egg.

WEEK TWO

GOALS FOR THIS WEEK

- Including as large a variety of nutritious vegetables as possible.
- Learning techniques to "sneak" in vegetables.
- Further reducing sugar, especially in soft drinks.
- Introducing new drinks.

SHOPPING LIST

Green and yellow vegetables (fresh or frozen—not canned) such as zucchini, spinach, parsley, peas, green beans, peppers, cucumbers, celery, sweet potatoes, butternut squash, pumpkin, carrots. Other vegetables your child likes can be added.

Canned tomato sauce, tomato paste (unsalted)

Sweets: Pure maple syrup, juice-sweetened jam

Seasonings: Any fresh or dried herbs, Mrs. Dash or comparable no-salt seasoning (without chemicals), chili powder, dried onions or onion powder, garlic powder, paprika, tamari soy sauce

Nonfat dry milk powder

Plain yogurt, preferably a brand such as Brown Cow, which contains acidophilus cultures

Cheese: Cream cheese, cottage cheese, unsalted cheddar, Monterey Jack, muenster, etc.

NOTE: If your child is lactose intolerant, do not serve him cheese; yogurt is all right.

Tofu (soybean curd) vacuum packed, soft or firm

Rice cakes and crackers (whole wheat or a combination of unbleached white flour and whole wheat; rice)

Replace any items from Week One shopping list that have been consumed.

ITEMS TO DISCARD

- All packaged and loose sugar (white, brown, raw)
- Canned vegetables
- Canned fruits in light syrup
- All processed meats and cheeses

Vegetables

As you have probably surmised by now, vegetables have a key position in the Eating for A's Program. In no other food category can one find the concentration of so many of the vital vitamins and minerals needed for optimum brain function. If you are like most parents, getting your child to eat vegetables can be a nightmare. There are many reasons for children to have an aversion to vegetables and it is unrealistic to think you will be able to talk them out of it at this point. If you are fortunate in having a child who likes particular vegetables, by all means take advantage of this by serving them as often as possible. But, in general, it is a major challenge to get the essential vegetables into his diet. This is where your prowess as a "sneak" will pay off.

Vegetables can easily be sneaked into soups, sauces, meat loaf, chili, fish cakes, hamburgers, turkey or chicken burgers, and sandwich spreads. The recipes in this chapter will provide you with some basic guidelines. After that, your own creativity will take over and vegetables will no longer be a challenge—they will be fun.

The snack items for this week also feature vegetables. Most of them are more straightforward (translated: not sneaky) and offer an opportunity for children to get involved.

Drinks

This is the week we start getting serious about what your child is drinking. Last week, you introduced "healthy" sodas which are in the "good" category. Now you're ready for better, which means limiting all commercial soft drinks to one every other day. If you think this is drastic, take this little quiz:

How many teaspoons of sugar are in a 12-ounce bottle of Coca-Cola? 1. 1–2   2. 2–4   3. 4–6   4. 6–8

The answer is none of the above. There are actually 9 teaspoons!

This is also true of most other soft drinks. Isn't this reason enough to work toward eliminating *all* soft drinks as soon as possible?

For the present, you can start replacing some of those denied sodas in the following ways:

Homemade Soda: Combine in a blender ⅔ cup of unsweetened fruit juice (grape, apple juice or cider, pineapple, orange), ⅓ cup of plain soda (seltzer), and some ice cubes. Blend well and serve. Add frozen dessert such as nondairy "Rice Dream" to make a mock ice-cream soda. If your child complains that the drink is not sweet enough, you can add a *small* amount of sugar or honey. This is not ideal, but at least you're the one controlling the sugar intake.

Shakes: Made with a base of fresh milk and/or nonfat dry milk powder, plain yogurt, soy milk or soy milk powder (particularly helpful for a child who is lactose-intolerant). Ingredients are optional; you can use any fruit or berry, combine fruits (bananas and oranges go well together), or add dried fruits such as dates or apricots for extra sweetness. Although most fruits are sweet enough, while you're "weaning" your child off sugar, you may have to add some honey or other sweetener. When using ice cubes, add them gradually. Smoothies can be refrigerated for a few days.

1. Strawberry Shake: Blend 1½ cups nonfat dry milk, 2 cups fresh or frozen strawberries, 1 teaspoon vanilla extract, 1 cup water, and ice cubes (optional).
2. Banana Delight: Blend 2 bananas, 1 cup plain yogurt, and 1 teaspoon of vanilla extract.
3. Peanut Smoothie: This is a great way to "sneak" in un-

sweetened peanut butter. Blend 2 cups milk, ⅓ cup peanut butter, ½ teaspoon of cinnamon, 2 teaspoons honey, and ice cubes (optional).

Juice Frosties: Made from a base of juice, either alone or in combination with nonfat dry milk.

1. Orange Frosty: Blend 1 6-ounce can frozen orange juice, 1 cup nonfat dry milk, 1 cup water, 1 teaspoon of vanilla extract, and ice cubes (optional).
2. Apple Quencher: Blend 1 cup apple juice, 1 peeled banana, 1 peeled orange, pinch of cinnamon, and/or ½ teaspoon vanilla extract.
3. Pineapple Punch: Blend 1½ cups pineapple juice, 1 large cubed carrot, and ice cubes. (Don't mention the carrot!)

This is just a sampling of drinks that are delicious, filling, and nutritious. The possibilities are practically limitless, and you (and your child's) imagination and creativity can make this an exciting adventure. Most of these drinks are in the "better" category. In Week Four there are recipes for even more nutritious ones, such as nut milks; in Week Six there is a discussion of juicer drinks.

Water: Don't neglect it. Water is an important nutrient and its function as a cleanser cannot be replaced by other drinks. If possible, have "good" water on hand all the time. Bottled spring water is good, but filtered water is even better and in the long run more economical and less trouble. Encourage your child to drink as much water as possible. To make it more interesting, add a small amount of juice or a squeeze of fresh orange or lemon. Water drinking is a good habit to get into.

Milk: Preferably low-fat or nonfat; no chocolate [carob syrup or powder (see p. 186) may be substituted].

Herbal Teas: There are many delicious noncaffeinated herbal teas which can be drunk hot or cold, plain, with a bit of honey, or mixed with fruit juice or milk.

Menus—Week Two

BREAKFAST

Follow the guidelines in Week One.

For pancakes, waffles, and French toast, serve syrup in the following way: Empty a bottle of regular pancake syrup. Then combine half of this syrup with half pure maple syrup. Return the mixture to the bottle so that no one knows what you've done! Do the same thing with jam: half sugar-sweetened jam, half fruit-sweetened jam.

LUNCH

SANDWICHES

Continue using ½ slice of unbleached white and ½ slice of whole wheat bread. Vary breads—use whole wheat pita (pocket bread), which is also available in mini sizes. As you are discarding all processed meats and cheeses, sandwich fillings should consist of unprocessed cheese, tuna, chicken, turkey (without skin), meat loaf, peanut butter (if necessary, combine half sweetened peanut butter with half un-sweetened,) jam, sliced eggs, or egg salad.

Raw vegetables: Lunch is a perfect meal to increase vegetable consumption. Here are some ways:

Raw vegetable accompaniments to sandwiches and soups: Children can participate in cutting up carrot sticks, green pepper rings, cucumber sticks, cherry tomatoes, celery, and broccoli or cauliflower florets. These can be served plain or with a dip (see p. 116).

Vegetable kabob: Place chunks of raw vegetables and hard cheese on skewers (fruits can also be used).

Finely chopped vegetables: carrots, celery, green peppers as well as alfalfa sprouts added to tuna, egg, chicken, or turkey salad to increase vitamin and mineral content.

Stuffed vegetables: Celery stuffed with chicken or turkey salad, egg salad, tuna, cottage or cream cheese, peanut butter; *Lettuce leaves* filled with any sandwich filling, then rolled and secured with a colorful toothpick; *Potatoes (white or sweet)* filled with chicken or turkey salad, tuna, grated or cubed cheese, vegetables such as chopped broccoli, peas, creamed or chopped spinach. To prepare: Bake potatoes, scoop out and mash insides and combine with fillings. Stuff the skins with the mixture and place in the oven or microwave to warm. Cheese or paprika sprinkled on top is festive.

Rice cakes or whole wheat crackers: Crackers can be spread with cottage cheese, cream cheese, peanut butter, or jam. These can be decorated with pieces of vegetables or fruits. (Younger children can make "faces" using raisins or carrot rounds or half cherry tomatoes for eyes; cucumbers, celery, green or red peppers for nose and mouth; alfalfa sprouts for hair.)

SOUPS

Soups are always a favorite with children. They can either be homemade or commercial. If you are going to use commercial soups or soup mixes, try to avoid canned ones (which are lower in vitamin content and usually contain large quantities of salt) and any mixes with artificial ingredients, flavorings, colorings, preservatives, sugar (by any name), and particularly MSG. Soups are an ideal way of sneaking in vegetables (see p. 104 and Week Two vegetable recipes). Store-bought soups can be enhanced by the addition of vegetables, either pureed or in chunks.

DINNER

APPETIZER

Fruit or vegetable juice (rich in vitamin C; when these are on the same menu with nonanimal foods high in iron, the iron is better absorbed), canteloupe cup (see p. 111).

Soups: Chicken, turkey, or vegetable such as Forest Vegetable (see recipe, p. 114) or Sunshine Vegetable (see recipe, p. 113)

MAIN COURSES

Turkey / Veggie Burger (see recipe, p. 111)
Spaghetti, macaroni, or lasagna with Sneaky Tomato Sauce
      (see recipe, p. 115), or other tomato sauce
Chili
Roast or broiled chicken or roast turkey
Salmon or other fish cakes (made with vegetables such as
      carrots, celery, potatoes)

VEGETABLES

Potatoes (white or sweet), preferably fresh and unpeeled;

should be baked, sautéed, or steamed. Avoid deep-frying (particularly avoid frozen French fries).

Any green or yellow vegetable, fresh or frozen, steamed, stir-fried, sautéed, or baked. See Nutrient Values List (p. 253) for important vegetables.

Salads (recipes for specific salads appear in Week Six, p. 157).

METHODS OF COOKING FRESH VEGETABLES

- Use a plastic or natural bristle brush to scrub vegetables; avoid peeling to retain vitamins in or under the skin.
- Use little or no water. Most of the important water-soluble vitamins (C and the B vitamins) in vegetables will end up in the water. Unless you are making a soup, they will be lost. Boiled vegetables are usually the least appetizing. If you have water left over from cooking vegetables, refrigerate it and use it as a base for future soups and sauces.
- Steam vegetables in a small amount of water in a heavy pan on the stove or in the microwave; or use a stainless-steel basket or bamboo steamer. For this method, bring a small amount of water to a boil in a saucepan with a lid (water should not be high enough to touch vegetables), place vegetables in the steamer, lower the heat and cover. Do not add salt. Cook until tender, but not soft.
- Stir-fry (cut in small pieces) or sauté in a small amount of oil until tender yet crisp (see recipe, Week Two).
- Bake alone or in casseroles.
- Do not use baking soda to retain color in vegetables; use lemon juice instead.
- Serve vegetables immediately after cooking to prevent vitamin loss.

SNACKS AND SNACK SUBSTITUTIONS

All lunch items can be used as snacks and snack substitutions for dinner. Continue using snack recommendations from Week One. Include yogurt, plain or with unsweetened fruit.

DESSERTS

Fresh fruit, whole or as a mixed fruit cup (concentrate on citrus fruits, papaya, strawberries, apricots, peaches, prunes, bananas).

Baked apple (fill with chopped nuts, raisins, a little honey, and cinnamon; omit sugar).

Cooked or raw applesauce

WEEK TWO

Recipes

TURKEY/VEGGIE BURGER
SERVES: 4

> *1 pound ground raw turkey (preferably dark meat)*
> *2 to 3 carrots, grated*
> *½ onion, chopped fine**
> *½ green pepper, chopped fine**
> *1 to 2 stalks celery, chopped fine**
> *1 teaspoon Spike seasoning (available in natural food
>   stores) or other favorite seasoning*
> *Canola oil or mist for frying*

1. Mix ground turkey, vegetables, and seasoning together.

---
*Use processor if possible.

2. Form into small burgers and fry in oil until well done on both sides.

Variations:
1. Broil or bake instead of frying, with or without a sauce (see p. 155 for sauce recipes). Oil can be omitted.
2. Use same recipe to make a Turkey/Veggie Loaf. (See meat loaf recipe, p. 129, for directions). Top with tomato or other sauce.
3. Experiment with other grated or chopped vegetables; refer to Nutrient Values List on p. 253 for substitution ideas.

Mom's Squash Pancakes

YIELD: 6–8 MEDIUM-SIZE PANCAKES

This is a delicious change of pace from potato pancakes, with a real nutrient boost. Don't tell what's in them until they've been eaten!

> *1 large butternut squash, peeled and grated*
> *1½ tablespoons whole wheat flour*
> *½ tablespoon toasted wheat germ*
> *2 eggs, well beaten*
> *Salt and pepper to taste*
> *Canola oil for frying*

1. Combine all ingredients except oil and mix well.
2. With moistened hands, roll into balls; then flatten into pancakes.
3. Heat oil and place pancakes carefully in skillet.
4. Fry until well browned—about 10 minutes on each side. Drain on paper towels or uncoated brown paper.
5. Serve hot, plain or topped with a bit of yogurt or maple syrup.

SUNSHINE VEGETABLE SOUP
SERVES: 4
This uses a base of yellow vegetables.

> *2 leeks,* white and green parts, washed well and*
> *chopped*
> *3 garlic cloves, chopped*
> *1 tablespoon canola oil*
> *1 cup sliced carrots (approx. 2 carrots)*
> *1 cup cubed peeled acorn squash*
> *2 sweet potatoes, cubed*
> *1 cup chopped spinach, fresh or frozen*
> *4 cups boiling water or stock*
> *Tamari soy sauce*
> *Salt and pepper to taste*

1. Sauté leeks and garlic in oil in a large pot until golden.

2. Place all vegetables in boiling water, cover and cook over low heat until tender, about 30 minutes.

3. Strain out vegetables, reserving cooking water, and puree in blender or processor.

4. Add vegetables to cooking water, stir well, season and heat through.

Variation: This basic soup may be varied by using different seasonal yellow vegetables such as corn and butternut or summer squash. It can be used as a stock for other soups or sauces. With the addition of tomato juice or pureed tomatoes, it looks like tomato soup—a great favorite with children, even those who wouldn't even look at a tomato. (If you're adding tomatoes, omit the spinach; otherwise it becomes too muddy-looking.)

---

*Onions may be substituted for leeks, but leeks are milder.

FOREST VEGETABLE SOUP

SERVES: 4

This uses a base of green vegetables.

> 2 onions, chopped
> 2 garlic cloves, minced
> 1 tablespoon canola oil
> 2 zucchini, chopped
> ½ pound green beans, cut in small pieces
> 2 celery stalks, cut in small pieces
> 1 cup chopped spinach, fresh or frozen
> ½ bunch parsley, chopped
> 2 tablespoons chopped cilantro (optional)
> 4 cups boiling water or stock
> Tamari soy sauce
> Salt and pepper to taste
> Juice of 1 lemon

1. Sauté onions and garlic in oil in a large pot until golden.

2. Add remaining vegetables and boiling water. Cover and cook over low heat until vegetables are soft, about 30 minutes.

3. Strain out vegetables, reserving cooking water, and puree in blender or processor. Return vegetables to cooking water, stir and heat through. Add seasonings and lemon juice.

Variation: You may substitute other green vegetables like green peppers, cucumbers, sweet peas, etc. If your child is put off by the color, add some potatoes or noodles to take his mind off it. You can also make this a cream soup with the addition of cream, milk, or blended tofu or nut milk (see p. 142, Week Seven Cream Soup recipe).

Tomato cannot be mixed into this soup without it becoming muddy, but you can experiment with ways to temper the "greenness," if necessary, with some yellow vegetables.

SNEAKY TOMATO SAUCE
YIELD: 1½ QUARTS

> *1 medium zucchini, chopped very fine**
> *2 carrots, chopped very fine**
> *1 red pepper, chopped very fine**
> *2 cloves garlic, pressed*
> *1 tablespoon olive oil*
> *2 cups tomato sauce, homemade or good quality jarred*
> *1 small can tomato paste*
> *1 teaspoon oregano, dried*
> *1 teaspoon basil, dried*
> *2 teaspoons crushed leaves or powdered thyme*
> *Crushed red pepper or cayenne to taste (optional)*

1. Sauté vegetables in olive oil until tender.

2. Combine tomato sauce, tomato paste, vegetables, and herbs in a heavy saucepan. Bring to boil, cover, and reduce heat. Simmer until vegetables are fully cooked (about one hour), stirring often (tomato sauce tends to burn at the bottom).

NOTE: You can add a small amount of milk at the end of cooking to reduce the "acidy" taste.

Variations: You can add or substitute other vegetables for taste and nutrient value (see Nutrient Values List, p. 253) but be careful not to include too many greens, as they will make the sauce look muddy. Be sure to include tomato paste and thyme, because of their nutrient content (see Nutrient Values List, p. 253).

---

*To fully disguise vegetables, puree sauce when cooked in a food processor.

TASTY DIPS FOR VEGETABLES

Cottage Cheese Dip
YIELD: 1 CUP

> 1 cup low-fat cottage cheese
> 4 tablespoons plain low-fat yogurt
> herbs such as chopped or dried parsley, thyme, oregano,
>   etc.
> spices such as chili powder, curry powder, etc.

Put cheese through a strainer, add yogurt and any herbs or spices you wish. You can also add salt or tamari soy sauce.

Yogurt-Peanut Dip
YIELD: ¾ CUP

> ½ cup plain low-fat yogurt
> 4 tablespoons natural peanut butter (no sugar or hydro-
>   genation)
> 2 teaspoons lemon juice
> Salt and pepper to taste

Mix well and refrigerate until ready to serve.

Variations: You can replace yogurt with soft tofu or use half yogurt, half tofu. For a quick seasoning, use a package of dried onion soup mix (without MSG). Crushed garlic, tamari soy sauce, and tahini (sesame butter) are good with tofu dips.

WEEK   THREE

GOALS FOR THE WEEK

- Familiarizing yourself with natural foods (possibly shopping in a natural food store or co-op).
- Eliminating sugar from the breakfast entirely.
- Introducing natural "fortification" into dishes.

SHOPPING LIST

The shopping list for this week will be longer than usual, since you will be stocking up on a variety of specialized, natural foods needed for the remaining weeks of the program. Most of the packaged and dry foods you purchase this week will last for a long time—either at room temperature or in the refrigerator or freezer. For that reason, you may want to buy in quantity. (See Storage on p. 82 for details.) The more perishable items will be used in recipes this week and replaced as needed. You may be able to purchase some items in the supermarket, but do some careful label reading to make sure you're getting the same quality.

This chapter provides you with a comprehensive overview of natural food items. Naturally you do not have to buy everything mentioned; in fact, you will probably only buy some things and use these pages as a reference for future weeks. Do buy the items marked with an asterisk (*), which you need for fortifying dishes during this week.

As you become more familiar with natural foods, you may find sources other than your local natural food store. If you are doing the program with others (neighbors, friends, relatives), you may want to investigate, at a future date, buying some items in bulk, thereby considerably reducing the cost.

NATURAL FOOD STORE

Nuts: Raw, unsalted almonds, cashews, peanuts, filberts, hazelnuts, peanuts, etc.

Seeds: Raw, unsalted sunflower, pumpkin, sesame, flax (can be made into a tea or used in baking; very high in Omega-3 oil). Seed meal, made from grinding seeds, which can be substituted for bread crumbs, flour, etc., as a binder. (You can also make your own seed meal in a small grinder.)

Natural sweeteners (Must be used in moderation): Honey (pure, uncooked, and unfiltered), pure maple syrup, malt syrup, brown rice syrup, brown rice powder, unsulfured blackstrap molasses, date sugar. Beware of any sugar which purports to be "natural"—it's still sugar and should be avoided.

Dried fruit: Although you can purchase most dried fruit in a regular store, you are now ready for the kind in the "best" category—those packaged without any preservative such as sulfur dioxide, no artificial coloring, and no additional sweetener (be careful of items like banana chips, which even in a natural food store may have added sugar).

Nut butters: Raw, salt-free, and sugar-free peanut*, almond, cashew, hazelnut, sesame (tahini).

Flour: Stone-ground 100 percent whole wheat, soy, rye, corn, buckwheat. (In addition to baking, uses for flour include thickening of sauces, pancakes, waffles, crepes, etc.)

Powder: Soy milk, nonfat dry milk*.

Grains: Brown rice*, barley (hulled or unhulled), groats (kasha), millet, bulgur, couscous, wheat kernels (berries), whole oats, quinoa. Pastas made from whole wheat, buckwheat, corn, soy, artichoke flour, etc.

Bread: A natural food store offers a greater variety of breads and the assurance of high nutritional quality. Breads in the "better" category can be found here.

Cereals: A vast array of natural cereals is available. Be sure to check the label: some have turbinado or brown sugar and should be avoided. Buy only one or two types of cereal for this week.* (See Breakfast.)

Eggs: Organic eggs are recommended. These are produced by free-ranging hens, without antibiotics and chemically treated feed.

Oil: We recommend cold-pressed unrefined oils. The only two you really need are olive and canola. The last is lowest in saturated fat and high in Omega-3 fatty acids. Both can be purchased in supermarkets.

Soy products: Tamari* (naturally aged soy sauce), regular, wheat-free, or low-sodium; miso (soybean paste—can be used in soup, sauce, or spreads (see recipe, pp. 143–44); tofu (soybean curd, of which many varieties are available; comes in soft and firm consistencies). Tofu in sealed packages is higher quality and more hygienic than loose tofu. Tempeh (fermented soybean curd) is usually sold frozen; choose any of the varieties available and keep frozen before using. Some of these items will not be used until later in the program, but it's good to familiarize yourself with them.

FATS FROM GOOD TO BAD

Since foods rich in saturated fat have been implicated in heart disease and some cancers, the Eating For A's Program recommends a diet low in saturated fat, and higher in polyunsaturated, unsaturated, and monounsaturated fats. Of particular benefit is a type of polyunsaturated fat called "Omega-3 fatty acids," found in abundance in many ocean and fresh water fish, edible linseed oil (from flaxseed oil), and canola oil.

Recommended oils rich in polyunsaturates are:

safflower oil (78 percent)   sunflower oil (64 percent)
soybean oil (61 percent)   corn oil (62 percent)

Olive oil, popularly used for cooking in Mediterranean countries, is very rich in monounsaturated fat (77 percent) and low in polyunsaturated fat (9 percent).

Foods rich in the less desirable saturated fat are:

chocolate (60 percent)   most cuts of red meat
mayonnaise (80 percent)   butter (80 percent)
peanut butter (50 percent)

Dried beans: Although dried beans are available in supermarkets, if you should want the less common ones (such as aduki, red lentils, etc.) you will find them in the natural food store. Dried beans are discussed as complementary proteins in Week Four.

Seaweeds: Edible sea vegetables are a treasure house of valuable trace minerals. Although seaweed is usually an acquired taste, it can easily be sneaked into foods. The most common are nori (a recipe for Nori Chips which is a potato

chip substitute that kids love can be found on p. 130),
wakame, kombu, and dulse. There are also seasonings made
from seaweed. The most delicious is Sesame Sprinkle or
Eden Shake, made from a combination of sesame seeds and
nori flakes. These can be sprinkled on everything from salads
to sandwich spreads to soups.

"Convenience" foods: You may be surprised at the scope
and versatility of natural foods, both packaged and frozen,
that are practically ready to eat, either "as is" or with the
addition of water or eggs. As these have no preservatives and
usually contain highly nutritious ingredients, they do not fall
into the same category as most processed food. Explore the
shelves and pick out some to try, alone or in combination with
other foods. They may be well accepted by your child, and if
so, will save you a lot of time and effort. Convenience food
labels usually specify the amounts of nutrients they contain.

Fresh vegetables and fruit: Some natural food stores sell
organically grown fresh produce. If the claim is reliable (and
you should check the sources of the produce to determine
this), the food has been grown without chemical fertilizers
and is not treated with preservative sprays or wax. We feel
that there is a distinct difference in taste and nutrient value in
organically grown produce, but it is usually more expensive
(particularly in areas distant from the farms) and does not
always look as appealing. Therefore, the choice is entirely up
to you.

*Miscellaneous: Flakes or grits from wheat, barley, rice, or
soy* are excellent for adding to soups, casseroles, cereals, etc.
They are quick-cooking and nutritious. Follow the directions
on the package. *Rice polish, rice bran, and raw bran* can be
added to baked goods, etc., for necessary fiber. Rice polish
contains nutrients as well. *Nutritional yeast (brewer's or*

torula) is nature's "wonder drug" because it contains many nutrients in a natural state. Buy the de-bittered kind. By itself, it may not have a pleasant taste, but when added to other food, it becomes undistinguishable (see Fortification, p. 125). The most palatable brand we've found is Red Star from Milwaukee, Wisconsin. *Wheat germ* is the heart of whole wheat; it comes in both raw and toasted* form and can be added to a multitude of dishes to increase their nutritional value. *Fruit juice concentrates* are excellent substitutes for sugar in drinks, desserts, and baked goods. There are many varieties: black cherry, apple, apricot, cranberry, etc. Use sparingly as they are very concentrated. *Arrowroot* is a natural thickener for sauces or soups and can be used to replace cornstarch. *Agar-agar* is a tasteless gelatin made from seaweed and should be used for gelatin dishes (see recipe for Kanten, p. 131). *Carob powder or syrup*, made from a pod, is a natural, unsweetened substitute for chocolate in drinks, snacks, and baked goods. *Grain beverages* are coffee substitutes, but you will be using them in future weeks as flavoring and coloring for sauces. *A variety of drinks* are made from flavored soy milk or rice extract. Our favorite is *Amasake*, made from rice and almonds, which is amazingly sweet, considering that it contains no sweetener. *Frozen desserts* include those made from soy or rice. As they resemble ice cream, they may be used as a treat, but be careful at this early stage to make sure your child knows that they are *not* ice cream.

STORAGE

General information on storage was discussed in Chapter 5; what follows is specific to items purchased from a natural food store.

Raw nuts and seeds: Can be kept out if they are going to be eaten within a few days; for any longer period, refrigerate. If you're buying in large quantities, keep only the immediate supply out and freeze the rest; then remove just enough for a two-day supply.

Nut butters: Store at room temperature (inverted occasionally so that the oil will mix in) until opened; afterward in the refrigerator.

Soy products: Store tamari in the pantry; miso at room temperature until opened, then wrap and refrigerate; store tempeh in the freezer for future use (see recipe for Marilyn's Curried Tempeh, page 170).

Whole grains, cereals, and flours, because they have no preservative, tend to go rancid or get "buggy" and should be refrigerated in sealed glass or plastic containers. Flour, in particular, should be kept refrigerated by the store selling it.

Dried fruit: Store in the refrigerator.

Whole grain bread: Store in the refrigerator or freezer for later use.

Menus—Week Three

BREAKFAST

Follow the guidelines in Week One.

The exception this week is that no refined sugar should be added to cereals, pancakes, etc. Instead, use the following natural sweeteners:

For cold cereals: Pieces of fresh fruit (bananas, strawberries, etc.) or dried fruit, particularly raisins, apricots, dates; small amount of date sugar; toasted wheat germ. (Tip: Grind wheat germ fine in the blender; it will look like brown sugar.)

For hot cereals: Dried fruit, maple or rice syrup, vanilla extract, cinnamon, fruit concentrate, toasted wheat germ.

For pancakes or waffles: Small amount of vanilla extract, cinnamon, honey, maple or rice syrup; add fruit or fruit concentrate to batter.

Do not discuss these substitutions with your child. If you have time, place all cereals in bowls in advance; use only pure maple syrup, but you can continue to serve it in a commercial syrup bottle; add items like wheat germ to the cereal box without anyone seeing you!

As for other breakfast items, start cutting down on items like bacon, replace fried or scrambled eggs at least once this week with poached or boiled eggs (to reduce the fat content). Hard-boiled eggs can be deviled by scooping out yolks and mashing with a small amount of mayonnaise and curry powder; replace the mixture and sprinkle with paprika. If your child is accustomed to having bacon or sausages for breakfast, try grilling rather than frying; better still, begin cutting down on the amount. One good way is to make a bacon omelet using small pieces or Bacon Pancakes (see recipe, p. 128).

Use *only fruit juice or honey-sweetened jam on toast.* If your child still misses the sweetness he had become accustomed to, make fruit cups or melon cups instead of serving plain fruit or fruit juice.

Fortification of breakfast food is discussed on page 126.

LUNCH

Follow menu ideas discussed in Week Two.

You may still want to make sandwiches half white and half whole wheat, but use the "better" whole grain bread. Use leftovers from dinner such as Fortified Meat Loaf (see recipe, p. 129) cold turkey or chicken (preferably dark meat or half white, half dark meat). Be liberal with tuna and salmon salads and sardines (skinless and boneless are more acceptable) because of the density of learning nutrients in them.

DINNER

FORTIFICATION

Dinner menus this week feature "fortified" foods.

An item rich in a necessary nutrient or multiple nutrients but difficult to get a child to eat by itself can be used as a natural fortifier. Some natural fortifiers are:

Dry milk of soy powder: diluted if a liquid is required or used as powder for the following dishes: mashed potatoes, creamed soups or creamed spinach, scrambled eggs (approximately one tablespoon per egg), hot cereal (combine dry powder with grain, then add water as usual).

Wheat germ, raw or toasted: can either augment flour or replace it in recipes (see Ingredient Substitutions, p. 185); sprinkle on cold or hot cereals, fresh fruit cups.

Nutritional (brewer's, torula) yeast: can be added to loaves, casseroles, hamburgers, baked goods, drinks. A good-tasting one like Red Star can give a surprising cheesy taste to popcorn.

Whole wheat, soy flour: can be added to or replace flour in any recipe (see Ingredient Substitutions, p. 185).

Rice bran or polish: can be added to hot cereals, loaves, casseroles, or baked goods.

Rice, barley, wheat, soy flakes: best used in soups, as a thickener, mixed in cooked cereal or grain dishes, or in casseroles.

Other natural fortifiers are discussed on p. 185, but the ones above were chosen for use in this week because they can be "sneaked" in recipes and are not detectable. See Nutrient Values List (p. 253) for the specifics of each of these fortifiers. Do not overdo amounts at first, because you want fortfication without detection. Spicy and strong seasonings (curry or chili powder) help disguise these fortifiers even more. See this week's sample recipes for some specifics.

DINNER

APPETIZERS:

See Week Two; try doing your own fortification such as adding wheat or barley flakes to one of the featured soups.

MAIN COURSES

Fortified Meat Loaf* (see recipe, p. 129)
Hamburgers/chicken or turkey burgers
Breaded chicken breasts
Stuffed peppers
Fish dishes
Any item from previous weeks; try doing your own fortification

VEGETABLES

Confetti Potato Salad (see recipe, p. 129)
See Week Two

DRINKS

Continue serving drinks from previous weeks. Allow commercial soft drinks only once a week.

NEW SNACK ITEM

Nori chips (see recipe, p. 130)
Continue serving snacks from previous weeks.

DESSERTS

Fresh fruit
Kanten (see recipe, p. 131)
See previous weeks.

WEEK THREE
Recipes

BACON PANCAKE
SERVES: 4

> *½ pound lean bacon, chopped*
> *¼ cup whole wheat flour*
> *1 egg*
> *½ cup low-fat or soy milk*

1. Fry bacon until almost crisp. Remove from pan and drain.

2. Mix all remaining ingredients well but not too long (there should be some lumps in the batter).

3. If you need more oil, spray pan lightly with canola mist (see p. 187). Spread bacon evenly on bottom of pan and then pour batter over it. Cook until batter is set and bottom is browned; then turn over and cook on other side.

4. Cut into wedges and serve.

An excellent way to fortify chopped beef is to grind in high-nutrient organ meats such as heart, lung, kidney, and calves liver with lean beef. Have the butcher grind a large amount, then freeze it in small batches and use the mixture in any chopped beef dish such as hamburgers, stuffed peppers, tomato sauce with beef, etc. No one will guess.

FORTIFIED MEAT LOAF
SERVES: 4

1 small onion, chopped
1 tablespoon vegetable oil
½ pound lean ground beef
½ pound ground dark meat turkey
2 tablespoons toasted wheat germ
1 small can tomato paste
½ cup water
½ tablespoon brewer's yeast
1 tablespoon sesame seeds
1 egg yolk, lightly beaten
1 tablespoon chopped parsley
1 teaspoon ground dried red chilies
Salt and pepper to taste

1. Preheat oven to 350 degrees.
2. Sauté onion in oil until golden.
3. Combine remaining ingredients and mix well.
4. Bake in a greased loaf pan for about an hour; top should be well browned (increase heat at end, if necessary).

CONFETTI POTATO SALAD
SERVES: 4–6

1 pound (3 large) potatoes, peeled, cooked and cut into
    small chunks
1 red pepper, chopped fine
1 green pepper, chopped fine
1 carrot, chopped fine
2 tablespoons (or less) mayonnaise (preferably
    homemade, or commercial without sugar—
    available in natural food stores)

lemon juice, if desired
1 teaspoon dried thyme
1 teaspoon prepared mustard
Pepper to taste

1. Steam vegetables lightly or leave raw, depending on preference for crunchiness.

2. Combine mayonnaise and seasonings.

3. Add mayonnaise to vegetables and toss all gently. Refrigerate until ready to serve.

NOTE: Using lemon juice will allow you to cut down on the amount of mayonnaise.

FRUITY NUT BUTTER
YIELD: 1 CUP

½ cup unsweetened applesauce
½ cup unsweetened apple butter
1 tablespoon toasted wheat germ
2 tablespoons unsweetened peanut butter (or other nut butter such as almond, sesame tahini, hazelnut, etc.)

Blend applesauce and apple butter together; then add wheat germ and nut butter and blend until smooth. Refrigerate for later use; it will keep for a week.

NORI CHIPS
Nori is a black seaweed sold in dried sheets in natural food and Oriental stores (it is usually less expensive in the latter). It is most commonly used to wrap around rice in sushi dishes. Although it may appear very exotic, nori makes a delicious snack alternative to potato chips. Children love it.

Nori sheets
Vegetable oil
Salt (optional)

1. Place one sheet of nori on a piece of aluminum foil, spread lightly with oil, then place another one on top. Continue doing this for as many sheets as you want.

2. Roll sheet in foil gently and let stand until oil is absorbed.

3. Remove from foil and sprinkle with salt if desired. (Seaweed is naturally salty, so you may find this unnecessary.)

4. Heat a pan and toast sheets lightly on top of stove until crisp (color will change from black to dark green). To make chips, cut into any size or shape you like. Cool and serve, or store in a closed container to keep crisp.

KANTEN

SERVES: 6–8

This is a nutritious alternative to Jell-O. Although the gelatin agar-agar is derived from seaweed, it is virtually tasteless and will pick up the taste of anything it is mixed with. Agar-agar can be purchased in natural food stores..

1 cup water
2 cups apple juice or other fruit juice
2 bars (6 tablespoons flakes) agar-agar
2 pints fresh strawberries (add sweetener if desired)
1 banana

1. Bring water and juice to a boil, add agar-agar and stir until dissolved.

2. Add strawberries and cook over low heat until fruit is cooked (about 15 minutes).

3. Pour mixture into blender with banana and blend until smooth.

4. Pour into mold dishes and refrigerate. When thoroughly chilled and set, slice into portions with a sharp knife. You can decorate the top with more fresh strawberries.

Variations:
1. Tahini Kanten is a custard made from agar-agar. Add 2 tablespoons tahini (sesame butter) and 1 teaspoon vanilla extract and blend in as in step 3. If you want to, you can omit the fruit.
2. Many other seasonal fresh fruits can be used instead of strawberries, or you can use frozen or dried fruits, or a combination. Experiment with fruits and fruit juices for both flavor and color.

WEEK FOUR

GOALS FOR THIS WEEK

- Introducing concept and use of complementary proteins.
- Using more grains for breakfast.
- Adding fortification with nuts and seeds.
- Using fewer soft drinks with sugar.
- Introducing nut milks.

SHOPPING LIST

If you did not purchase these in the previous week, do so now:

Amazake (sweet rice drink)
Brown rice

Barley malt (from natural food store)
Raw cashews (from natural food store)
Sunflower seeds (hulled) or sunflower seed meal
Packaged tofu (soft)
Pumpkin seeds
Wheat germ
Raw almonds
Rolled oats
Dried soybeans
Dried or canned kidney beans
Natural peanut butter (nonhydrogenated, no salt or sugar)

ITEMS TO DISCARD

- All commercial soft drinks
- All products containing white flour
- White rice

WHAT ARE COMPLEMENTARY PROTEINS?

Growing children have a major need for protein foods because they are the building blocks of the body. We are most familiar with animal protein—meat, fish, poultry, dairy products, and eggs. These are known as complete proteins because they contain all eight of the essential amino acids which the body cannot produce itself and must obtain from food. Nonanimal foods are also sources of protein. These include whole grains and grain products, seeds, nuts, dried peas and beans (tofu, the curd made from cooked soybeans, is a particularly high-powered and versatile protein source).

Vegetable proteins have the advantage of having no cholesterol and little saturated fat, with few exceptions. They are less adulterated than protein foods from animals, which are pen-reared, and often contain hormones, antibiotics, and other chemicals. Vegetable protein foods are excellent fortifiers. They also give you a chance for more variety and versatility in menus.

Most vegetable protein sources are called incomplete because they do not contain all eight essential amino acids by themselves. They must be combined with other proteins to be complete; they then become complementary.

For example, a grain such as brown rice may be lacking the necessary amount of one or two amino acids, whereas a legume (dried bean or peanut) may contain the missing one(s). If the two are combined at the same meal, the result is a complete protein. In general, only strict vegetarians have to be concerned with this. If your child is eating a meal that features vegetable protein and also includes dairy products, eggs, and/or even a small amount of meat or fish, he is probably getting more than enough complete protein. But there may be times or circumstances (such as allergies) when you want to serve only vegetable protein dishes, and it is good for you to know how. It's really easy—all you have to do is make sure there is more than one vegetable protein food at the same meal. Practically every culture boasts a particular

EXAMPLES OF COMPLEMENTARY PROTEIN COMBINATIONS

Rice, barley, or wheat berries served with lentils, kidney beans or garbanzo beans
Peanut butter on whole wheat bread
Bean tacos
Bean soup served with whole wheat crackers spread with tahini (sesame seed paste)
Lentil salad served with whole wheat pita
Pasta and beans

complementary protein dish such as rice and beans; corn tortillas and refried beans; humus (chick-pea spread) and pita bread; and minestrone soup.

Vegetable proteins can be included in any meal, and in every course, even in drinks! This week's menus and recipes feature a variety of them. With these and the information in the Nutrient Values List (p. 253) as your guides, you can go on to create many of your own delicious complementary protein dishes.

Menus—Week Four

BREAKFAST

Follow the menus in previous weeks. In addition, this week features new grains for breakfast, such as cereals made in a thermos, soy waffles, and two kinds of super energy pancakes. Any breakfast grain product can be enhanced by the addition of sunflower or sesame seeds; whole wheat toast spread with a spoonful of natural peanut butter constitutes an excellent complete protein.

LUNCH

Follow the menus in previous weeks. New sandwich fillings in Week Four recipes include humus (chick-pea spread) and tofu "cream cheese" and tofu/peanut butter.

These can also be used as snack substitutes for dinner.

DINNER

APPETIZERS

Follow the menus in previous weeks. In addition, serve vegetarian "chopped liver" (made with 8 ounces of mushrooms, 2 onions, 3 cups of walnuts, and 2 hard-boiled eggs (all chopped and mixed together), and minestrone (vegetable, bean, and pasta soup).

MAIN COURSE

Tofu/Meat Hamburgers (half tofu, half chopped meat)

Vegetarian Chili (using your favorite chili recipe, omit meat, substitute an equal amount of bulgur wheat, any chopped vegetables you wish and more chili powder)

Oriental Rice With Salmon (see recipe, p. 139), Halibut, etc.

Nut loaf (see recipe, p. 140)

Casserole combinations (grains, beans, and vegetables; grains and cheese, seeds and grains, etc.)

Soyburgers—Natural food stores sell many mixes and frozen meatless burgers.

VEGETABLES

Follow the menus in previous weeks.

DESSERTS

Follow the menus in previous weeks.

Brown Rice Pudding (see recipe, p. 142)

DRINKS

This is the week for eliminating the last one of your child's soft drinks. But, as you've been gradually "weaning" him off them, it may be less traumatic than you think. Make sure he's getting plenty of other tasty liquids: juices, homemade sodas, shakes, smoothies, milk and water. In addition, introduce nut milks (see recipe, p. 142).

SNACKS AND SNACK SUBSTITUTES

Healthy "Crackerjacks" (see recipe, p. 144)

Plain popcorn

Frozen bananas (Peel and freeze whole, then slice into thin pieces; or roll whole banana in crushed nuts and carob syrup and freeze again, if desired.)

WEEK FOUR

Recipes

SOY WAFFLES
SERVES: 4

> *1 cup soybeans, soaked for 6 hours*
> *1½ cups rolled oats*
> *1 tablespoon canola oil*
> *2¼ cups water*

1. Place all ingredients, except water, in food processor and process until smooth; then add water.

2. Lightly grease waffle iron, pour small amount of batter on it, and cook until browned.

3. Serve hot with yogurt, fruit, maple syrup, honey, or fruit-sweetened jam.

BROWN RICE
YIELD: 1 CUP RAW RICE YIELDS APPROXIMATELY 3 CUPS COOKED

Brown rice should be a staple in your pantry. Because you will be using it so much, it is essential that you cook it well. As all brown rice, regardless of where it is purchased, is unprocessed, it must be thoroughy washed to remove all surface dirt, soil, etc.

1. Place raw rice in a large bowl and cover with cold water. Then rub it briskly between your hands as though you were washing clothes. Pour it through a sieve or colander and repeat the process as many times as it takes for the water to come out clean. You will be amazed! The effort is well worth it once you see how "white" the rice becomes.

2. Place rinsed rice in a heavy saucepan and add a little less than twice the amount of cold water or broth (e.g., 1 cup of rice to 1¾ cups of water). Bring quickly to a boil; then lower heat and cover. Do not stir! Stirring causes rice to get mushy.

3. Cook until water is absorbed, remove cover and let stand for a few minutes before serving.

Variations:

1. *Dry-toasting:* You can toast rice without oil, which makes it firmer and quicker-cooking and gives it a nutty taste. To do this, place in a pan over high heat and stir continuously for about 5 minutes or until color is darker and there's a nutty aroma.

2. *Sautéing:* Rice to be served as a separate dish, such as pilaf, can be sautéed first in a little oil or butter, with seasonings, onions, garlic, mushrooms, or other vegetables (if desired). Sauté until golden, about 7 minutes, stirring continuously, then add water or broth and cook as above.

ORIENTAL RICE WITH SALMON
SERVES: 4
This recipe uses packaged Walnut Acres Oriental Rice Mix, which contains excellent ingredients and is naturally easier to prepare.

>*2 cups Oriental rice mix*
>*4 cups water*
>*2 stalks celery, sliced thin*
>*1 onion, diced*
>*2 cups soybean sprouts*
>*½ pound mushrooms, sliced*
>*1 red pepper, diced*
>*1 green pepper, diced*
>*¼ cup chopped fresh parsley*
>*½ to ¾ pound fresh salmon, diced fine*
>*1 teaspoon tamari soy sauce*
>*1 small can water chestnuts (optional)*

1. Add rice to water, bring to a boil, and cook, covered, for 20 minutes or until done.

2. Place vegetables on top of rice, cover, and steam for 10 minutes.

3. Add salmon, cover, and steam for five minutes or until fish is cooked.

Variations: You can use chicken, turkey, or other fish high in learning nutrients (see Nutrient Values List) instead of salmon. Other vegetables such as carrots, broccoli, spinach, or kale can also be used. If desired, vegetables and fish can be stir-fried instead of steamed.

BASIC NUT LOAF
SERVES: 6–8

> *1 pound onions, cut in large chunks*
> *¼ pound mushrooms, chopped fine*
> *1 green pepper, chopped fine*
> *1 celery stalk, chopped fine*
> *1 tablespoon canola oil*
> *1 cup whole wheat bread or cracker crumbs*
> *½ cup wheat germ*
> *1 pound nuts, ground fine (can be cashews, almonds,*
> *   and hazelnuts, or cashews alone)*
> *1 tablespoon brewer's yeast*
> *1 tablespoon dried sage*
> *½ tablespoon dried thyme*
> *Tamari soy sauce, salt, and pepper to taste*
> *2 eggs, beaten*
> *1 cup (or more) low-fat or soy milk*

1. Sauté vegetables lightly in oil.

2. Combine with other ingredients and place mixture in a greased loaf pan. Bake at 325 degrees for 45 minutes to 1 hour until done but still moist. Heat can be raised at end to brown top.

3. Serve plain or with Sneaky Sauce Tomato or Brown Sauce (see pp. 115, 155)

Variations: You can replace bread crumbs with cooked grains such as brown rice; other vegetables can be substituted. Adjust liquid for moist consistency.

Basic Hot Cereal
SERVES: 2–3

    2 cups water
    1 cup rolled oats (noninstant)
    2 tablespoons raisins or other dried fruit
    Cinnamon

1. Bring water to a boil; slowly add rest of ingredients.

2. Cover pan and cook over low heat until water is absorbed, about 15 minutes.

Variations:

1. *Other grains* can be added to or substituted for oatmeal. For example: try using whole oats (which need to be soaked and will take longer to cook), or millet or bulgur. Also, you can add fresh fruit such as a banana, seeds such as sunflower or sesame, or nuts.

2. *Thermos Cereal:* A really easy way to make hot cereal is in a wide-mouthed thermos. For one serving, pour in ⅓ cup of hot water and 2 tablespoons of cracked wheat (Wheatena); tighten the lid and let stand anywhere from a half-hour to overnight. Before serving, you can add cinnamon, honey, milk, and dried or fresh fruit. Other grains such as couscous, bulgur wheat, and even rice (if you soak it in hot water first) can be made in a wide-mouthed thermos—great for trips and picnics.

Brown Rice Pudding
SERVES: 2–4

> *1 cup cooked brown rice*
> *1 container (or enough to cover rice) almond-flavored soy malted (Westbrae brand, sold in natural food stores) or Amazake, a drink made from sweet brown rice*
> *½ teaspoon vanilla extract*
> *Dash cinnamon*

Combine all ingredients in an ovenproof dish and bake in 350 degree oven for 30 to 40 minutes.

Variations: Combine cooked brown rice with fresh or canned chopped pineapple, dried fruit, chopped nuts, and sweetener such as maple syrup, honey, fruit juice concentrate, etc.

Nut "Milk"
There are many commercial drinks made from rice or soy in the natural food stores, but another highly nutritious drink is a "milk" made from nuts. Nuts are so valuable because of their protein and calcium content, but they are sometimes difficult to digest. Nut milk takes care of that—and is also delicious. It's very rich, so it should be served sparingly; nutritionally, a little goes a long way.

Use raw nuts (there is a substantial loss of vitamin B_1— thiamin—when nuts are roasted or fried) such as cashews, almonds, hazelnuts, etc. (see Nutrient Values List, p. 253, for details). Cashews and almonds are the most popular for "milks." If using cashews, be sure to wash them well in warm water and rinse until water is clean. Then put them in a food processor with the desired amount of water and liquefy thoroughly. A good proportion is 1 part nuts to 3 parts water.

Bring mixture to a boil and cook for about 15 minutes for greater digestibility. You can add sweeteners, vanilla, fruit, etc. Cool before serving; refrigerate for longer use.

A quick way to make nut "milk" is to liquefy nut butter (cashew, almond, etc.) in water, sweeten to taste, and serve.

Nut "milks" are excellent for making nondairy dishes like Mock "Cream" Carrot Soup (see p. 179 for recipe).

TWO SANDWICH SPREADS
YIELD: 1 CUP

Tofu "Cream Cheese"

> *1 cup soft tofu*
> *1½ tablespoons canola oil*
> *½ teaspoon salt (optional)*
> *½ to ¾ tablespoon honey*
> *½ tablespoon tamari soy sauce (for salty flavor) or*
> *vanilla extract (for sweet taste)*
> *Lemon juice (optional)*

Blend all ingredients until *very* smooth. Allow to stand several minutes before serving. Can keep in refrigerator for up to a week.

NOTE: If you want a whiter color, try adding 1 teaspoon of liquid lecithin (available in natural food stores) before blending.

Variation: You can add chopped dates, walnuts, or vegetables like scallions—anything that would go into regular cream cheese.

Tofu/Peanut Butter

Mixing soft tofu with peanut butter not only "stretches" peanut butter in terms of money and calories but makes it a better protein source. All you have to do is blend the tofu with peanut butter in whatever proportions feel right (up to half and half), add some tamari soy sauce (for color as well as flavor) or fruit juice and serve. Don't tell—no one will be the wiser.

HEALTHY "CRACKERJACKS"
YIELD: ABOUT 20 CUPS

> *½ pound natural popcorn (with no salt or oil)*
> *½ cup raw peanuts*
> *Barley malt to cover*

1. Combine popcorn and peanuts. Spread evenly on lightly oiled baking tray and cover with thin layer of barley malt.

2. Bake at 325 degrees until malt is melted, about 10 minutes.

3. Remove from oven, shake lightly to mix, and allow to cool. Store in closed container to keep dry.

7

THE SECOND MONTH

If you have followed the program strictly, you should see some of the following results: increased concentration, greater calmness, more energy directed to achieving tasks, clearer skin, healthier-looking hair, better sleeping habits. Because you see your child on a daily basis, it may be difficult to observe the more subtle changes. But this is a good time to ask yourself if your child doesn't seem a little calmer and generally more alert. Also, listen to what he's saying about the program. What are his complaints? Does he miss his old foods? Is he becoming more comfortable with the dietary changes?

Keep up the good work.

Because this is a gradual program, you may not be able to assess concrete results until the end of the third month, but you are laying the groundwork now for that payoff.

W E E K   F I V E

GOALS FOR THIS WEEK

- Eliminating all snacks containing white sugar.
- Increasing the consumption of high energy foods such as pasta and pizza.
- Increasing the consumption of vegetables by preparing them in different ways.

SHOPPING LIST

Whole wheat or 7-grain English muffin
Whole wheat pita bread
Whole wheat flour
Firm tofu
Grated cheese
Eggs
Vegetables: onions, leek, garlic, carrots, sweet potato, asparagus, bok choy (Chinese cabbage), red and green peppers, spinach, mushrooms (dried shiitake, if possible)
Grain coffee (Pero, Cafix or Postum, found in natural food store)
Arrowroot powder
Soya Kaas (mozzarella-type soy "cheese," found in natural food store)
Tomato sauce or puree
Brown rice syrup (found in natural food store)

Handling Sugar Withdrawal

This is the week in which all sugary snacks are eliminated. It is not unusual for a person to experience symptoms of withdrawal when sugar consumption is drastically reduced or eliminated. Symptoms may include irritability, headaches, lethargy, fatigue—in fact, many of the same symptoms that accompany withdrawal from coffee or cigarettes. But the primary symptom is usually more frequent hunger, even hunger shortly after eating.

The best way to handle all symptoms is to feed your child more often. Be prepared to feed him five times a day, making the snacks more substantial than usual. If you serve the right kind of foods, you can keep his calories up (without adding pounds) and offset the desire for minimally nutritious sweets.

High energy foods are the key at this crucial time. And the best high energy foods are complex carbohydrates, which are body builders without steroids. Complex carbohydrates include grains such as rice and wheat, beans, seeds, nuts, and vegetables like potatoes. These foods are filling and provide staying power because the body derives energy from them over a long period of time. The following items should be served as often as possible:

Plain or stuffed baked potato

Whole wheat, spinach, or any other kind of nonwhite flour pasta, plain, with tomato sauce, or with vegetables (go easy on the fattening elements such as high-fat cheese and butter)

Pizza is excellent for satisfying hunger and for high energy. Pizza often suffers a bad reputation as a junk food but it is really the opposite when it is made with the right ingredients (whole wheat crusts, low-fat cheese, vegetables). This week features some easy pizza recipes for snacks or main courses.

New Ways with Vegetables

You have been a sneak long enough! But no matter how well you did it, you couldn't sneak in the quantity of vegetables your child needs to bring his RDAs to the optimum levels. Now is the time to increase vegetable consumption, and your child should be ready to accept vegetables in their natural form. You will probably still need to go slow, but there is much you can do. Even children who "hate" vegetables will usually eat them in a Chinese restaurant. Using this as a tip, choose the vegetables your child likes best and instead of disguising them, try stir-frying them. You will probably have more success at first if you combine them with thin slices of beef, poultry, or fish, but you can experiment with other interesting combinations too.

Another way to cook favorite vegetables is to steam them until tender but still crunchy, and then serve them with a tasty sauce or sprinkled with Parmesan cheese.

See recipes on pp. 150–54 for some ways to serve vegetables.

Menus—Week Five

BREAKFAST

Follow the menus in previous weeks, but concentrate on foods high in complex carbohydrates (see complementary protein list, Chapter 6, Week Four, which includes such foods). Examples: Serve whole grain waffles, pancakes, breads (or toasted sandwiches), cereals, etc. Serve animal protein dishes (eggs, meat, cheese) no more than twice this week.

LUNCH

Follow the menus in previous weeks. Use as many complex carbohydrates and vegetables as possible. Some good ideas are: tabouli in whole wheat pita pocket bread or baked potatoes stuffed with vegetables.

DINNER

APPETIZERS

Follow the menus in previous weeks.

MAIN COURSE

Follow the menus in previous weeks.
Pizza
Basic Stir-Fried Vegetables (see recipe, p. 150) with
    Chicken/brown rice (see recipe, p. 137)
Fish cakes with Brown Sauce (see the recipe, p. 155)
Tofu "Meat" Balls (see recipe, p. 152)

VEGETABLES

Kathy's Super Spinach (see recipe, p. 153)
Couscous with Peas
Steamed zucchini with Parmesan cheese
Green beans and almonds in Miso/Tahini Sauce
    (see recipe, p. 155)

SNACKS AND SNACK SUBSTITUTES

See previous weeks.
Ann's Shapely Cheese Crispies (see recipe, p. 156)
Prunes or dates stuffed with peanut butter

DRINKS

Follow the suggestions in previous weeks.

Hot carob milk (1½ cups of low-fat milk, ½ cup of water, ½ teaspoon of vanilla extract, 4 teaspoons of honey, 1 tablespoon of carob powder, 1 tablespoon of black-strap molasses)

WEEK FIVE

Recipes

BASIC STIR-FRIED VEGETABLES

SERVES: 4

Here's a recipe we know from experience is a favorite with children. You have an almost unlimited choice of vegetables for stir-frying, but in terms of learning nutrients, the ones in this recipe are preferred. Naturally, you can add any others for taste. Try not to have too many, as the flavors compete with one another.

> *2 tablespoons canola oil*
> *1 onion, chopped or sliced thin*
> *1 leek, sliced thin*
> *2 garlic cloves, minced or pressed*
> *½ cup sesame seeds*
> *2 stalks broccoli (stems chopped fine, and flowers left whole)*
> *2 carrots, chopped fine*
> *1 sweet potato, chopped fine*
> *2 asparagus stalks, chopped fine*
> *1 cup shredded bok choy (Chinese cabbage)*

1 red pepper, chopped fine (green can be substituted but
red will lend a touch of color)
1 cup chopped or torn spinach
1 cup chopped or sliced mushrooms (dried shiitake
mushrooms are preferred because they're higher in
some of the learning nutrients)
Tamari soy sauce
Herbs as desired

1. In a wok or deep frying pan, heat oil and add onion, leek, garlic, and sesame seeds. Stir with a wooden spatula or wok utensil continuously to brown; be careful not to burn the garlic.

2. Add "hard" longer-cooking vegetables, such as broccoli stalks, carrots, sweet potato, and asparagus. Stir continually over high heat for about 5 minutes.

3. Add remaining vegetables and continue stirring for another 10 minutes.

4. Add tamari and other seasonings and a bit of water if vegetables are very dry; cover and lower heat. Cook only until vegetables are done but still firm (slightly crunchy). Serve plain or with brown rice or noodles.

NOTE: The purpose of stir-frying is to cook quickly over high heat in order to seal in the juices of the vegetables. This is accomplished by frying all sides of the vegetables, which is why it is important to stir continuously. If the heat is high enough and you work quickly, you will not need any additional oil for frying. Although this recipe looks like you have to do a lot of preparation, you can save time by cutting the vegetables in advance and packing them in separate plastic bags. In this way, you can prepare several meals' worth of vegetables at the same time and just quickly stir-fry them when needed.

Variations: You can use sunflower and/or pumpkin seeds, but sesame seeds are a must because they offer a variety of learning nutrients (see Nutrient Values List, p. 253). You can also use alfalfa, mung bean, or soybean sprouts; add at the end of cooking so that the enzyme content will be preserved. You can change the taste considerably by the kind of seasonings you use. This recipe is essentially Oriental, but you can make it sweet and sour (with a touch of lemon or vinegar and molasses), Indian (with curry powder), or Mexican (with chili powder or, even better, hot red chilies). You can also add beef, chicken, turkey, seafood, or fish; if using uncooked ingredients, stir-fry at the same time as the vegetables; if adding already cooked ingredients, do so at end of the cooking time.

Although this recipe will not work with frozen vegetables alone, you can combine frozen and fresh vegetables. Just make sure you drain as much water as possible from frozen vegetables and add them at the end, as they require very little cooking.

TOFU "MEAT" BALLS
YIELD: 6 TO 8 "MEAT" BALLS

> 1 pound firm tofu
> 2 eggs
> ½ cup seasoned bread or cracker crumbs
> ¼ minced onion
> 2 garlic cloves, pressed
> ½ teaspoon dried oregano
> ½ teaspoon dried basil
> black pepper to taste
> 3 tablespoons grated cheese
> 1 quart tomato sauce, homemade (see p. 115) or good
>   quality commercial

1. Preheat oven to 350 degrees.

2. Process or blend tofu and eggs until smooth.

3. Add remaining ingredients, except tomato sauce, and mix well.

4. Form into balls. If mixture does not hold together, add more bread or cracker crumbs, wheat germ, seed meal, or any other binder.

5. Place in a baking pan and cover with tomato sauce. You can sprinkle more grated cheese on top if you wish.

6. Bake for about 20 minutes or until fully cooked.

NOTE: If you prefer, these can be fried in a small amount of olive or canola oil. Add tomato sauce at end.

KATHY'S SUPER SPINACH
SERVES: 3–4

> *1 cup poppy seeds*
> *1 tablespoon canola oil*
> *1 pound fresh spinach, well-washed and chopped or*
> *shredded*
> *tamari soy sauce and honey to taste*

1. Toast poppy seeds lightly in oil.

2. Add spinach, stir gently until wilted, and then add seasonings. Cover for a few minutes.

3. Serve immediately.

NOTE: Do not dry spinach after washing; the water is needed for cooking.

STEAMED VEGETABLES

Steaming is certainly the best way to prepare vegetables to conserve their nutrients. Steamed vegetables are delicious and highly acceptable to children if you do not overcook them and serve them with something interesting. Here are some ideas.

The following vegetables are excellent steamed in either a collapsible or bamboo steamer or a pressure cooker:

> *Potatoes, white or sweet*
> *Broccoli*
> *Cauliflower*
> *Zucchini (really quick)*
> *Carrots*
> *Hard squash such as butternut or acorn, sliced*
> *Asparagus*
> *Corn on the cob*

Toppings

> *Small amount of melted butter, margarine, or vegetable oil*
> *Toasted sunflower or pumpkin seeds*
> *Chopped nuts such as almonds, cashews, or peanuts*
> *Grated cheese, particularly Parmesan*
> *Tomato sauce (see p. 115)*
> *Brown Sauce (see p. 155) or other sauces*
> *Sweet and sour sauce*
> *Honey or maple syrup (for carrots, sweet potatoes, butternut or acorn squash)*

Brown Sauce
YIELD: 1 QUART

Most prepared sauces and gravies contain MSG, other additives, and too much salt. You're better off making your own.

> *1 onion, chopped*
> *1 tablespoon butter or canola oil*
> *2 cups water or vegetable stock*
> *2 tablespoons grain coffee substitute, such as Pero,*
>   *Cafix, Postum (unsweetened)—needed for color*
> *½ cup arrowroot powder*
> *2 tablespoons tamari soy sauce*

1. Sauté onion in butter or oil.

2. Add 1 cup of water or stock, bring to a boil and simmer gently for about 15 minutes.

3. Add grain coffee and blend well.

4. Dilute arrowroot powder in remaining water and add slowly, stirring continuously.

5. Add tamari and stir. Serve hot over grains, vegetables, poultry, nut loaves, beans, etc.

Miso/Tahini Sauce
YIELD: ½ CUP

> *1 tablespoon miso (soybean paste)*
> *2 tablespoons tahini (sesame butter)*
> *1 teaspoon grated orange peel*
> *1 tablespoon arrowroot powder or whole wheat flour*

1. Blend miso and tahini together and add orange peel.

2. Place in pan over low heat, combine with arrowroot or flour, and stir until thickened.

3. Add water (amount will depend on consistency desired) and stir well. Simmer until heated through and serve hot.

Variations: To make a lighter sauce, *substitute tamari soy sauce for miso.* To make a sandwich spread, *increase tahini to 4 tablespoons, omit arrowroot or flour, and add only 1 or 2 tablespoons of water. Cook 5 minutes until thickened. Cool and store in refrigerator.*

ANN'S SHAPELY CHEESE CRISPIES
YIELD: 12–15 STRIPS
This amount should tide 4 to 6 children over until dinner.

> ¼ *cup whole wheat flour*
> ½ *teaspoon baking powder*
> 2 *pinches of paprika*
> *salt to taste*
> 6 *tablespoons grated cheddar or Swiss cheese*
> 1 *tablespoon beaten egg*
> 1 *tablespoon low-fat or soy milk*
> *sesame seeds, optional*

1. Preheat oven to 350 degrees.
2. Combine flour, baking powder, paprika, and salt.
3. Add cheese, egg, and milk.
4. Mix ingredients together until dough forms a ball. If the dough seems too dry, add a bit more of the beaten egg.
5. If possible, refrigerate the dough for at least an hour to make it easier to roll. Sprinkle a little flour on the dough or onto a clean breadboard or counter. Roll dough until it is very thin, so that it will be very crisp when baked.
6. Cut the dough into fanciful shapes with cutters; or slice into thin strips.
7. Sprinkle sesame seeds on an ungreased cookie sheet, if desired. Then place dough on top of seeds.
8. Bake for 15 minutes or until crispies are lightly browned. Store in a tin or airtight container. Do not refrigerate or crispies will become soggy.

PIZZAS

There is a wide variety of commercially prepared nutritious pizzas available in natural food stores. But it's very easy to make your own either with prepared dough or on whole wheat English muffins, tacos, or pita bread. Simply spread with tomato sauce, add chopped vegetables (if desired) and top with shredded cheese or Soya Kaas (mozzarella-style soy "cheese"). A favorite with Dr. Schauss' children is pizza topped with pineapple slices. Broil in toaster oven or stove; microwaves are less successful, as pizza will not brown.

WEEK SIX

GOALS FOR THIS WEEK

- Emphasizing more raw goods such as salads; increasing the variety of salad items.
- Learning about the value of sprouts: How to use them and how to grow them
- Making salad dressings and involving your child in preparing salads and salad dressings.
- Introducing more snacks of raw foods.
- Continuing to serve more frequent meals or "mini meals."

SHOPPING LIST

Any of the following vegetables may be used in salads; romaine, red-tipped, or any other loose leaf lettuce (see Box), arugula, watercress, cabbage (green, red, white), tomatoes, cucumbers, zucchini, radishes, alfalfa, mung bean sprouts, carrots, celery, spinach, asparagus, green beans, peppers (green, red, yellow), cauliflower, broccoli, beets, endive, parsnips, scallions.

Eggs
Cottage cheese
Honey
Dijon mustard
Soft tofu
Canola oil
Apple cider vinegar
Lemons
Potatoes
Tempeh
Yogurt, plain nonfat
Raisins
Walnuts
Curry powder
Turkey
Calves liver
Whole grain or quinoa (in natural food store) or multi-colored (spinach, tomato) macaroni (spirals, ziti, or other interesting shapes)
Olive or canola oil
Dried or fresh herbs such as parsley, dill, oregano
Alfalfa seeds, mung beans, raw sunflower seeds, whole wheat berries (in natural food stores)
Tomato juice (salt- and sugar-free); unsalted ("better")
V-8 juice

Leafy lettuces are recommended because they are far more nutritious than head lettuces, such as iceberg. For example, romaine lettuce contains more vitamin A, calcium, and iron; soft head leafy lettuces contain 2 to 3 times more vitamin A, calcium, and iron. Head lettuce, in addition, has a much greater concentration of insecticide sprays.

A Word About Organically Grown Produce

When it comes to purchasing raw vegetables to be used for salads or homemade vegetable juices, we prefer organically grown produce. Purity is of greater importance when vegetables are not going to be heated. Vegetables classified as organically grown are grown without artificial fertilizers, pesticides, and other sprays and are not treated with preservative sprays or wax. There is a growing awareness of the value of organically grown produce, and, consequently, more is available. It is still advisable to check out the source and only buy from reliable markets. Organically grown produce is usually more expensive, but we feel it is worth it, both in taste and nutrition.

Why Raw Foods Are Important

Perhaps no matter how inventive you have been in disguising them, cooked vegetables have still been problematic for your child. Even if a child eats cooked vegetables, chances are there are some he prefers raw. This is not surprising; most children enjoy eating fresh, crisp, crunchy raw vegetables. And it's a good thing, because in addition to possessing all

DIETARY FIBER

Fiber in the diet plays an important role in maintaining a child's health, including weight management, regulation of blood lipids (fats), and maintenance of gastrointestinal activities (e.g., normal bowel movements).

Children can consume an adequate amount of dietary fiber by regularly eating a wide variety of nuts, legumes, whole-grain breads and cereals, fresh fruits and vegetables. At mealtimes, dietary fiber helps the "overeater" cut down on his calorie intake by making him chew more, promoting a sense of satiety ("fullness") while still eating, and slowing the transit time of foods through the gastrointestinal system. For those with elevated blood cholesterol levels, dietary fiber has been shown to lower blood cholesterol.

the benefits of cooked vegetables (see Week Five) some raw vegetables have unique properties:

- Certain vitamins, such as vitamin C, are better protected in the vegetables that contain them when the vegetables are raw. Cooking can destroy or diminish these vitamins.
- Raw vegetables contain larger amounts of fiber (see above for the role of fiber in the diet)
- Heating food also destroys various enzymes in vegetables. These enzymes aid digestion, particularly when eaten at the beginning of a meal.
- Raw vegetables can provide the body with extra protection from infection, because vitamin C, in particular, is considered a protective vitamin.
- Raw green leafy vegetables, in particular, are important, because of the chlorophyll which they contain.

■ Raw foods, when eaten regularly, are wonderful cleansers on the inside and the outside. This last benefit should be of particular interest to teenagers, who uniformly are concerned about bad skin. Salad (and raw vegetable juice) is good for the hair and skin. When they start caring about the opposite sex, teenagers start caring about what they look like. This is where you can "sell" salad to even the most resistant hold-out.

Tips About Salads

■ You will be inclined to serve salad more frequently if you prepare all the ingredients in advance. Tear lettuce and cut other salad ingredients, store them in separate tightly closed plastic bags, and wash and dry them just before serving. This prevents them from getting soggy and wilted.

■ Vegetables for salad require careful washing. For this you can use a solution of vinegar or salt and water, a mild non-detergent soap solution or (best) ½ teaspoon of Clorox to one gallon of water. For a Clorox bath, soak leafy vegetables and thin-skinned fruits for 10 minutes; root vegetables and heavy-skinned fruits for 15 to 30 minutes. Use a fresh bath for each group. Rinse in fresh water for 5 to 10 minutes. The advantages of this care is that fruits and vegetables will keep much longer and wilted ones will become crisp again; and, of course, the harmful sprays, etc., will have been removed.

One mother details the specific cosmetic advantages of raw foods and routinely reminds her almost-teenage daughter that if she wants to keep her beautiful clear skin, she has to eat salads. It works!

■ Vary shapes, sizes, and colors in salads. For example, top salad with grated zucchini, carrots, beets, or parsnips. This can be done quickly with the grating blade of the food processor.

■ It is our experience that many children prefer eating individual ingredients rather than an already tossed salad. They can also be fussy about salad dressing; in fact, salad is often preferred without any dressing at all. You may be more successful in getting your child to eat salad if you lay out all the vegetables on a tray or large plate, with dressings on the side, and let him create his own.

■ Garnishing salads with croutons (whole wheat, of course!) and bits of cheese will help a child develop a taste for salad.

■ Raw vegetables provide an excellent opportunity for child involvement. Encourage your child (at any age) to wash, tear, cut, grate, etc.; to create shapes and combinations of salad and dressing ingredients. With this "investment" in the food, he will be more likely to eat it.

Sprouting

Perhaps the best activity to interest children in is sprouting seeds, beans, and grains. Sprouts are the freshest, least expensive, most nutritious year-round vegetable you can have. True, many sprouts can be purchased, but it's easy and much more economical to grow your own.

Items for sprouting can be divided into the following categories:

Seeds: Alfalfa, sesame, sunflower, radish
Beans: Lentils, soybeans, mung beans, garbanzos (chickpeas)
Grains: Wheat berries, rye, corn, oats

Sprouting time will vary, as will the length at maturity. The information below gives you details on the most common sprouts.

HOW TO SPROUT

Beans, seeds, and grains for sprouting must be untreated and should be purchased in a natural food store. The easiest method for sprouting is to place the seeds, etc., in a glass jar and cover with water overnight. Pour out the water the next morning and rinse the seeds well. Do not keep seeds in direct sunlight. Turn jar on its side to distribute seeds evenly and keep moist by covering seeds with a wet cloth or paper towels. Rinse seeds 2 to 3 times a day (you can use mesh or cheese-cloth or a colander for easy rinsing) until sprouts are ready to eat. Alfalfa sprouts can be placed in a sunny window after the second day to develop a bright green color (chlorophyll).

Sprouts are ready to eat as follows:

Mung beans—¼ to ¾ inch high
Alfalfa—1 inch high
Soy and other beans—½ inch high
Chickpeas, lentils—½ inch high
Sesame and sunflower—when first sprout appears

The yield from sprouts may amaze you—1 tablespoon of alfalfa seeds will produce a quart jar of sprouts! Sprouts can last in the refrigerator for several days if they are rinsed and dried regularly. In addition to their place in salads, they can be cooked (lightly steamed or stir-fried) or used in baking (for instance, sprouted wheat, bread or muffins.)

Vegetable Juices

Freshly extracted vegetable juices have all the properties of raw salad, without the fiber. They can be consumed in addition to salads or as an alternative. Sometimes a child may be more inclined to drink rather than eat, and vegetable juice can give him the same nutrition and energy quickly and effortlessly. Also, because they are so filling, vegetable juices can be used as a snack or mini-meal.

To extract juice from vegetables you need an electric juicer. There are many brands available in different price ranges; you needn't spend a fortune. (Some are easier to clean than others, a quality you may want to look for.) The most important thing if you buy one is to have it accessible—if it's on the counter, you'll use it; if it's tucked away in the pantry, you won't bother. Many vegetables can be juiced; the most common are carrots, celery, and beets. Experiment with combinations; for example, apples go well with celery and carrots. Simply wash (see p. 161) and scrub the vegetable well, cut off the ends, and cut into pieces to fit the juicer. If you do not want to use a juicer, you can place vegetables in a blender with enough water to liquefy. However, this is different from extracted juice in that it will not be as smooth and will contain the fiber.

DILUTING JUICES

This is the week when your child can begin to get into the "best" category of drinks. Up to now, he has been (hopefully) drinking unsweetened natural fruit juice. However, fruit juice has a heavy concentration of fructose, and children tend to drink fruit juice liberally, filling up on it instead of food, and getting a big dose of fructose in the bargain.

For example, how many apples do you think it takes to make an eight-ounce glass of apple juice? Three and a half pounds! Can your child eat three and a half pounds of apples in one sitting? Of course not. But that's exactly what he is getting, without the fiber, when he drinks an eight-ounce glass of juice.

While you were weaning your child off sugar, it was necessary to give him that "zap" of fructose to compensate for the other sweeteners. Now he's ready for juice diluted with either water or herb tea. You can dilute it as much as is tolerable. By giving him this kind of drink, he will not have the excess fructose, which is stored as fat in the body, nor the common bloating that interferes with digestion.

Salad Dressings

There are limitless possibilities for salad dressings. They can range from something as simple as olive oil and vinegar or lemon to elaborate cooked ones with a long list of exotic ingredients. Your choices should be governed by your child's taste and the nutritional content of the ingredients. Natural food stores carry many prepared dressings in bottles or dry packets. Read the ingredients carefully before you purchase them to try out. We prefer to make our own both for reasons of quality and economy. Dressings are really easy, especially if made in a blender, and they keep well in the refrigerator, so large quantities can be made at one time. Also, if you make your own, you can sneak in avocados, tomatoes, and spinach—which might not be eaten otherwise. Let your child participate in making dressings; if he's old enough, he can invent his own. It's really fun. For some samples of dressing recipes, see pages 167–69.

> S omeone we know often puts pieces of apple in salads or coleslaw. Her children think it's some sort of prize and pick them out, thereby getting the benefit of the apples— and eating some cabbage in the process.

Menus—Week Six

BREAKFAST

Follow the guidelines for previous weeks, particularly Weeks Four and Five.

LUNCH

Follow the guidelines for previous weeks.

Include salads such as Turkey Vegetable Salad (see recipe p. 171), Marilyn's Curried Tempeh (see recipe p. 170), vegetable salads, raw vegetable pieces (crudités), and vegetable juices as much as possible. Make tacos filled with meat, cheese, or refried beans and topped with shredded letuce, tomatoes, and other vegetables. Add raw vegetables and sprouts to sandwiches and soups.

DINNER

APPETIZERS

Gazpacho (see recipe, p. 169)
Salads with dressings (see recipes, pp. 167–71)

MAIN COURSE

Follow the guidelines for previous weeks, particularly
   Weeks Four and Five.
Pasta dishes with vegetables, fish, chicken, or turkey
Surprisingly Good Liver (see recipe, p. 171)

SNACKS AND SNACK SUBSTITUTES

Follow the guidelines for previous weeks.
Peanut Butter/Honey Snacks (see recipe, p. 172)

W E E K   S I X

Recipes

MOSS'S SO-LOW MAYO
YIELD: 1 CUP
Here's a low-fat nutritious substitute for ordinary mayonnaise.

   1 egg, boiled or poached (until yolk is barely hard),
      cooled and chopped
   2 tablespoons lemon juice
   1 tablespoon honey
   1 teaspoon Dijon mustard
   1 cup 1% fat cottage cheese
   salt and pepper to taste

   Blend all ingredients until very smooth. Place in a tightly
covered glass container and refrigerate. It should keep for up
to a week.

*Variations: To make an herb mayonnaise, add 1 garlic clove
and 3 tablespoons of chopped fresh basil or 2 to 3 teaspoons of*

dried basil. To make Russian dressing, add catsup (made from honey) and relish.

Tofu Mayo

YIELD: 2 CUPS

A high-protein, low-fat, no-cholesterol substitute for mayonnaise. Tofu requires more seasoning, so be liberal with vinegar or lemon juice, and add herbs such as dill or thyme, and spices such as cayenne pepper, if necessary.

> *3 tablespoons canola oil*
> *2 tablespoons apple cider vinegar or lemon juice*
> *1 pound soft tofu*
> *¼ teaspoon honey*
> *½ teaspoon mustard*
> *salt or tamari soy sauce to taste*
> *2 garlic cloves, pressed, or 1 scallion, chopped*
>   *(optional)*

1. Add oil and vinegar or lemon juice in blender.

2. Slowly add tofu, blending continuously.

3. Add remaining ingredients and blend until very smooth. Add additional seasonings if desired and chill before serving.

Variations: Add ½ avocado for a nutritious green goddess–type dressing. Add 1 tablespoon of tahini (sesame paste). Increase the garlic and tamari to taste. To make a salad dressing, add extra oil and vinegar and/or lemon juice.

ANNA'S HONEY MUSTARD DRESSING
YIELD: ¼ CUP

> *1 tablespoon prepared mustard*
> *1 tablespoon honey*
> *Juice of ½ lemon*
> *1 tablespoon canola or olive oil*

Blend all ingredients well and use on greens, cooked vegetables, and fish.

QUICK GAZPACHO
SERVES: 4

This is actually a liquid salad that is most acceptable to children—especially on hot summer days.

> *1 green pepper, cut in chunks*
> *4 tomatoes,* cut in chunks*
> *½ cucumber, cut in half and unpeeled (if not waxed)*
> *1 small onion, cut in half*
> *6 garlic cloves, cut in half*
> *½ to 1 cup olive oil*
> *2 tablespoons apple cider vinegar*
> *3 hard rolls or slices of stale whole-grain bread soaked*
>   *in water until soft*
> *salt and pepper to taste*

1. Blend vegetables, olive oil, and vinegar in blender or food processor until smooth.

2. Squeeze water out of rolls or bread, add to mixture and continue processing until smooth. Add some cold water if soup tastes too strong.

3. Chill well and serve, garnished with croutons and pieces of scallion, cucumber and green pepper.

---

*To make this more liquid, use tomato juice (without sugar) or V-8 juice instead of (or in addition to) fresh tomatoes; you can reduce olive oil to adjust the amount of liquid.

COLESLAW

YIELD: 1 QUART

Even children who are finicky about eating salad will jump at coleslaw. So you can use the opportunity to add in other vegetables with the cabbage.

> *1 small head cabbage (green, red, or half and half), shredded**
> *1 tablespoon vinegar or lemon juice*
> *1 sweet (Bermuda) onion or several scallions, sliced thin*
> *2 carrots, grated* or sliced thin*
> *½ cup Moss's So-Low Mayo (see recipe, p. 167)*

1. Cover cabbage with water and a few tablespoons of salt and allow to stand for about a half hour. (This helps eliminate much of the "gas" from raw cabbage.)

2. Drain water, rinse off salt, and combine with remaining ingredients. Serve chilled.

Variations: You may add any combination of celery, parsley, dill, radishes, green and red peppers, pineapple, apples, raisins, sunflower seeds, peanuts.

MARILYN'S CURRIED TEMPEH

SERVES: 2–3

A good nonmeat substitute for chicken or turkey, tempeh is very high in protein, and low in fat.

> *8 ounces tempeh (available in freezer in natural food stores)*
> *2 tablespoons homemade mayonnaise (see p. 167)*
> *½ tablespoon plain nonfat yogurt*
> *1 tablespoon raisins*
> *1 tablespoon walnuts*
> *1 teaspoon curry powder*

---

*Easily done in food processor.

1. Steam tempeh for 10 minutes. Cool and cut into cubes.
2. Mix remaining ingredients well and pour over tempeh. Cover and refrigerate.

TURKEY VEGETABLE SALAD
SERVES: 3–4

> *2 cups cooked chopped dark meat turkey*
> *1 stalk celery, finely diced*
> *1 stalk broccoli, finely diced*
> *1 carrot, finely diced or shredded*
> *½ teaspoon powdered thyme*
> *1 garlic clove, crushed*
> *1 teaspoon tamari soy sauce or salt*
> *2 tablespoons homemade mayonnaise (see p. 167)*

1. Combine turkey and vegetables.
2. Combine seasonings and mayonnaise and toss thoroughly with turkey and vegetables.
3. Cover and refrigerate. Serve cold.

SURPRISINGLY GOOD LIVER
SERVES: 4

> *1 pound calves* liver*
> *1 teaspoon blackstrap molasses*
> *2 teaspoons tamari soy sauce*
> *1 tablespoon canola oil*
> *2 tablespoons whole wheat flour*
> *1 onion or leek, diced*
> *black pepper to taste*

---

*Calf is preferable to beef liver, bcause there is no buildup of toxins (liver is a repository for ingested chemicals) due to the youth of the animal.

1. Remove outer covering and hard parts of liver. Then cut into small pieces.

2. Mix molasses and tamari together and marinate liver in this mixture for about an hour.

3. Heat oil, remove liver from marinade, lightly coat with flour, and sauté *briefly* (about 5 minutes, on both sides. Overcooking makes liver tough; inside should be slightly pink.

4 Remove from pan. Heat a small amount of oil in the same pan and sauté the onion until golden. When cooked, add marinade and liver and heat through. Season with pepper.

5. Serve hot over rice or noodles.

PEANUT BUTTER/HONEY SNACKS
YIELD: 30-40 SMALL BALLS

With Tofu

>   1½ pounds firm tofu
>   1 pound peanut butter
>   2 tablespoons honey
>   ¼ teaspoon cinnamon
>   Peanuts, granola, or wheat germ

Blend all ingredients together. Divide into small balls, then roll in crushed peanuts, granola, or wheat germ. Place in freezer until frozen; serve as desired.

With Powdered Milk

>   1 pound peanut butter
>   3 tablespoons honey
>   ½ cup nonfat milk powder
>   1 tablespoon carob powder (optional)

Blend all ingredients together; add a little water or fruit juice if mixture doesn't stay together. Divide into balls and roll as in recipe on p. 172. You can also add chopped peanuts and press into a pan; slice into pieces and chill for at least an hour. Serve as desired.

WEEK SEVEN

GOALS FOR THIS WEEK

- Adding more grains for breakfast.
- Eliminating all white flour (only whole grain products; different grains).
- Emphasizing more poultry, fish, and shellfish.

SHOPPING LIST

Whole wheat flour
Rolled oats, other ingredients for granola (see recipe
    p. 182)
Whole wheat or 7-grain English muffins
Whole grain (or artichoke flour) pasta (in natural food
    store)
Millet, kasha (buckwheat groats), whole wheat couscous
    (see p. 119)
Quinoa (in natural food store)
Eastern oysters
Dark meat turkey
Plain soy milk (in natural food store)
Almonds, cashews, sunflower seeds

By this point in the program, you should have eliminated all white flour products, even unbleached white flour. In other words, your child is ready to eat bread in the "best" category. This is particularly important if you have a child who can't seem to get enough bread at meals; whole grain bread will give him much more protein, vitamin E, and fiber.

If you have a child who uses bread in a sandwich just as a way of handling food without getting his hands dirty, pita (pocket) bread is ideal—and this also comes in whole wheat. Or you can try your hand at making some easy breads or rolls (another great cooking adventure for kids).

HOMEMADE BREAKFAST GRAINS

An easy way to insure that there will be a variety of whole grains for breakfast is to make your own pancake or waffle mixes, and granola. This is a lot easier than it sounds and is certainly in the "best" category nutritionally as well as far more economical than buying commercial brands. Large batches can be made at a time and stored in either the refrigerator or the freezer. (See the recipes on pp. 100 and 128 and the variation to the pancake recipe in Week One.)

OTHER GRAINS

You can now get more adventurous with grains for lunch and dinner; one example is *quinoa* which is called "the Mother Grain" and has been around for over 5,000 years. Highly nutritious, quick-cooking, and light, it can substitute nicely for the grains you've been using.

MORE VARIETIES OF FISH

We have continually stressed the importance of fish and poultry (especially dark meat) for the valuable "learning nutrients" they contain. Now, you are ready to try some of the less usual kinds of fish. When someone first mentioned that her children actually *liked* oysters, it was hard to believe. But our taste tests have shown that it is possible—so we have included an oyster recipe because of the Eastern oyster's unusually high zinc content. Naturally, we don't expect that you will be serving oysters too often, but perhaps they can be an occasional addition because it's hard to get enough zinc through food.

The advisability of buying foods in season has already been pointed out. This is especially true with fish. We recommend that you buy the freshest fish you can get. When you buy fish that are in season, you will pay less and get more nutritionally.

Menus—Week Seven

BREAKFAST

Follow the guidelines in Week Five, but add items like Multi-Grain Pancakes (see recipe p. 101) muffins made from whole grains, nutritious quick breads, oat cakes, and Homemade Granola (see recipe, p. 182).

LUNCH

Follow the guidelines in Weeks Five and Six.

DINNER

SOUPS

Mock Cream Soup (see recipe, p. 179)
Chicken Soup with Giblets (see recipe, p. 178)
Fish Soup

MAIN COURSE

Favorite Oyster Chowder (see recipe, p. 177)
Turkey with Carrot Stuffing (see recipe, p. 180)
Barrett Burgers (see recipe, p. 181)
Other fish, broiled or baked
Pasta with clam sauce

VEGETABLES

Follow the menus in previous weeks.

GRAINS

Quinoa with Buckwheat (see recipe, p. 181)
Millet pancakes
Taboule (bulgur wheat salad made with chopped tomatoes,
    cucumbers, scallions; olive oil and lemon dressing)

SNACKS AND SNACK SUBSTITUTES

Snacks from previous weeks
"Juicicles" (pops made from pure fruit juice frozen with
    sticks for holding them; trays can be purchased)
Mock Danish Pastry (see recipe, p. 183)
Nut butters and unsweetened jam or raw vegetables on rice
    cakes

WEEK SEVEN
Recipes

FAVORITE OYSTER CHOWDER
SERVES: 4–6

> *1 quart fresh Eastern oysters**
> *1 small onion, chopped*
> *1 tablespoon canola oil*
> *1 cup white wine (this is optional but adds to the taste)*
> *10 ounces fresh or frozen spinach (thawed and drained)*
> *16-ounce can frozen potato soup*
> *1 cup low-fat or soy milk*

1. Rinse oysters well and chop into bite-size pieces.

2. In a heavy pot, sauté onion in oil until golden, add oysters, wine or juice, and simmer over low heat for about five minutes or until edges of oysters curl. Add spinach.

3. Add remaining ingredients; heat until warm but *do not boil*.

---

*Be sure to buy *Eastern* oysters, as there is a major nutrient difference between them and Pacific oysters.

CHICKEN SOUP WITH GIBLETS
SERVES: 6–8

> *8 cups water or stock*
> *1 tablespoon canola oil*
> *2 onions, cut in large pieces*
> *2 garlic cloves, chopped*
> *2 celery stalks, cut in large pieces (reserve leaves, torn)*
> *1 small (2- to 3-pound) chicken*
> *1 pound giblets**
> *2 carrots, chopped*
> *salt and pepper to taste*
> *2 tablespoons chopped fresh dill*

1. Bring water or stock to a boil. Meanwhile, in a separate pan, lightly sauté onions, garlic, and celery stalks until tender.

2. When water is boiling, add chicken and giblets, sautéed vegetable and carrots, and cook, covered, over low heat for about an hour or until chicken is tender.

3. Skim off fat from soup (cool if you have time; this makes the skimming process easier).

4. Remove giblets from soup and slice into small pieces; then return them to broth.

5. Add seasonings, celery leaves, and dill and heat through. Hopefully, the giblets will go unnoticed and get eaten along with the other ingredients. You can also make this soup with turkey giblets; it's an excellent use for leftover turkey.

---

*Giblets are an excellent source of some important learning nutrients; ask your butcher for the liver, heart, and gizzard.

Mock Creamed Carrot Soup
SERVES: 6

> *4 cups water or stock*
> *1 leek or large onion, cut in chunks*
> *2 cloves garlic, chopped*
> *2 tablespoons grated ginger*
> *1 tablespoon canola oil*
> *4 large carrots, cut in chunks*
> *1 sweet potato, cut in chunks*
> *1 cup raw cashew nuts*

1. Bring water or stock to a boil. Meanwhile, sauté leek or onion, garlic, and ginger in oil until tender.

2. When water is boiling, add carrots, sweet potato, sautéed vegetables, and cashews.

3. Lower heat, cover and cook over low heat until carrots and sweet potato are tender.

4. Allow to cool; then puree in food processor until smooth.

NOTE: The cashews make this a very rich soup, so you may want to dilute it with more water. You can use cashew butter if preferred; the amount will depend on the consistency you want.

Variations: This tasty soup is so much like creamed soup in color and texture that you will want to make it even if you are serving dairy products. However, it is a boon if you're not. There are countless variations: try other vegetables such as spinach, broccoli, cauliflower; add turkey or chicken, seafood or fish. Don't be afraid to experiment with other nuts like almonds.

CHICKEN OR TURKEY WITH CARROT STUFFING

SERVES: 6–8

1 roasting chicken or turkey (4 to 5 pounds)
salt and pepper to taste
1 tablespoon margarine or canola oil
2 small onions or 6 scallions, sliced thin
2 garlic cloves, minced
2 pounds carrots, sliced thin
1 teaspoon dried thyme
½ teaspoon dried tarragon
Juice of 1 lemon plus peel

1. Season cavity of bird with salt and pepper. In oil, sauté onions, garlic, carrots, ½ teaspoon thyme, ¼ teaspoon tarragon, and lemon peel, then add a little water and cover for about three minutes.

2. Fill cavity with vegetables and close opening with skewers or thread.

3. Roast at 325 degrees for 30 minutes.

4. Rub outside of bird with lemon juice and remaining herbs.

5. Continue roasting for another hour or more, until done. Add more lemon juice, if desired, before serving. Remove stuffing and serve separately.

BARRETT BURGERS
YIELD: 6–8 BURGERS
This is an excellent recipe for leftover rice and is a great complementary protein dish, chock full of learning nutrients.

>   2½ cups cooked rice
>   1¼ cups raw cashews
>   1¼ cups raw sunflower seeds
>   1 to 1½ cups water
>   1 to 2 teaspoons tamari soy sauce
>   2 large carrots, cut in large chunks
>   bunch of cilantro
>   5 garlic cloves
>   1 tablespoon grated ginger
>   Oat bran (enough to bind)

1. Place rice, cashews, and sunflower seeds in food processor and process until almost fine. Add water, soy sauce, and remaining ingredients and process until smooth.

2. Remove from processor and add enough oat bran to bind ingredients together, yet still keep the mixture moist.

3. With damp hands, form the mixture into flat patties, place on a lightly greased sheet, and bake at 350 degrees for one hour.

QUINOA WITH BUCKWHEAT
SERVES: 4
This is a change from rice—a light, quick-cooking dish featuring quinoa, called "the mother grain" because it is a close relative to one of the earliest, most nutritious grains.

>   ½ cup light buckwheat (groats, kasha)
>   1 cup quinoa
>   2 cups boiling water

1. Toast buckwheat in a heavy pan over high heat, stirring continuously for 5 minutes.

2. Add quinoa and toast for an additional three minutes.

3. Add boiling water, stir once, lower heat, and cover. Cook for about 8 minutes or until grain is done, yet firm. Add more water, if necessary.

4. Serve with applesauce, plain yogurt, or brown sauce (see recipe, p. 155)

Variation: This can also be served as a hot cereal for breakfast.

Homemade Granola

YIELD: 4 CUPS

Despite some expensive ingredients, this granola is both more economical and more nutritious than store-bought. You can make large batches and refrigerate or freeze it for later use. It can be used for snacks as well as for breakfast. Use sparingly—it's very rich.

> *3 cups rolled oats*
> *½ cup sunflower seeds*
> *¼ cup sesame seeds*
> *¼ cup canola oil*
> *½ cup chopped nuts (cashews, almonds, peanuts)*
> *½ cup honey*
> *1 teaspoon vanilla extract*
> *pinch of salt or tamari soy sauce*

1. Mix all ingredients together well and spread evenly on a cookie sheet.

2. Bake at 325 degrees for about 30 minutes, mixing occasionally to prevent burning.

3. Allow to cool, stir again, and place in airtight jars or containers.

Variation: For a delicious apple-crisp dessert, spread granola over sliced apples and bake for 30 to 35 minutes in a medium oven.

MOCK DANISH PASTRY
YIELD: 4 PASTRIES

> *2 eggs*
> *¼ cup low-fat milk or soy milk*
> *2 slices whole grain bread*
> *cream cheese or mock cream cheese (tofu) for spreading*
> *juice of ½ lemon*
> *1 teaspoon vanilla extract*
> *1 apple and 6 strawberries, chopped; or 6 pineapple chunks*
> *2 tablespoons raisins*
> *½ teaspoon cinnamon*

1. Heat oven to 400 degrees.

2. Beat eggs and milk together and saturate bread, as for French toast.

3. Lightly grease a baking pan and bake bread slices for 5 minutes. Then remove from oven.

4. Whip cream cheese, lemon juice, and vanilla together. Spread on each slice of bread.

5. Mix fruit and raisins. Place on top of each slice of bread, gently roll up slice, securing with a toothpick. Sprinkle cinnamon on top and bake for another 3 minutes.

6. Serve warm as is, or cut into small pieces.

WEEK   EIGHT

GOALS FOR THIS WEEK

Reintroducing desserts; sugarless desserts.
Substituting more nutritious ingredients in standard recipes.

SHOPPING LIST (Only for dessert ingredients)

Fruit concentrate (Mystic Lake brand, if possible, sold in
natural food stores)
Whole wheat pastry flour
Baking powder (nonaluminum)
Baking soda
Nutmeg, allspice, cinnamon
Applesauce, unsweetened
Eggs
Butter, canola oil
Honey
Orange juice, frozen; grape juice
Dry milk powder, nonfat
Dried fruit (raisins, dates, figs, apricots)
Nuts (almonds, cashews, sesame seeds)
Amazake (in natural food stores)
Carob chips
Carob powder
Arrowroot powder
Peanut butter
Pie crust, frozen (Oronoque Orchards brand, if possible,
because it contains no sugar and is very tasty)

The Second Month **185**

Granny Smith apples, oranges
Yogurt (nonfat, plain)
Sweetener (maple syrup, brown rice syrup, etc.)
Pumpkin or winter squash

Reintroducing Desserts

As we have been emphasizing throughout the book, it takes quite a while to "wean" a child off sugar. For this reason, and also to keep from confusing him, we have not included any desserts except fruit. By this time, your child should be fully aware of what the program consists of and what foods are unacceptable. If this is the case, he is ready for other desserts. The rationale for this is that he can now discriminate between less and more nutritious food and so when you give him a piece of cake, he will know it's not the same as the piece of cake in the corner luncheonette, even if it looks the same.

Some people feel that dessert is entirely unnecessary, and we are a part of that minority. But if you want to add dessert to the lunch or dinner menu, of course do so, with some moderation. Natural sweeteners are still sweeteners; they can easily take the place of more nutritious calories and therefore should be consumed in moderation. We are providing a variety of recipes for sweet things with the trust that you will not make all of them this week!

Substitution of Ingredients

No doubt by now you have already experimented with substituting some more nutritious ingredients for the ones called for in your favorite standard recipes. The following chart should help you to take care of all possible situations and it is our hope that it will greatly expand your menus.

After you become familiar with these principles, you will probably have no need to refer to it. At that point, you will have become a full-fledged Eating For A's cook!

INGREDIENT	SUBSTITUTION
1 cup white flour	1 cup minus 2 teaspoons whole wheat flour
1 cup sugar	1¼ cups date sugar; 1 to 1½ cups brown rice syrup powder; 1½ cups ground-up raisins, dates, or other dried fruit ½ to ¾ cup honey; 1½ cups molasses; 1½ cup apple, black cherry, or other fruit juice concentrate; 1 to 1½ cups brown rice syrup or Amazake rice drink
1 square chocolate	3 tablespoons carob powder + 2 tablespoons milk or soy milk (*Note:* carob can be used to replace cocoa in the same proportions)
Cornstarch, white flour (as thickeners)	Whole wheat flour or arrowroot (2 teaspoons combined with 1 cup cold water added to the liquid to be thickened)
Gelatin	Agar-agar (2 tablespoons flakes or 1 tablespoon granules diluted in 3½ cups hot water or juice; 1 bar to 3 cups liquid)

Whole milk	Soy milk (liquid or made from powder); nut milk (see p. 142)
Baking powder	Most commercial baking powders contain sodium and aluminum powders which can destroy certain vitamins and are hard to digest. Substitute nonaluminum type such as Rumford's sold in natural food stores; or make your own: 1 part baking soda, 2 parts cream of tartar, 2 parts arrowroot. Store in a tight jar and sift before using.
Salt	Lemon juice, herbs, spices, natural salt substitutes such as Mrs. Dash
Oil, butter	In *cooking*, sauté food in a small amount of water, broth, or juice instead of oil or butter; or use one of the nonstick sprays such as canola or olive oil mist (made by El Molino). In *baking*, use 2 tablespoons soy or other flour to 1 cup of water or juice.

SWEETENERS

When using liquid sweeteners such as honey, molasses, brown rice syrup, etc., reduce other liquids in the recipe and/ or increase the dry ingredients. Dry milk powder, in addition

FLOUR

In general, when substituting whole wheat pastry or other whole grain flour for white, you will probably have to increase the amount of liquid in the recipe. (A good addition, which will also lend sweetness, is the liquid from soaking dried raisins, dates, or other dried fruit.) In baking, don't make batters as thin as white flour batters and don't expect the end result to be as light and fluffy. If you're not using pastry flour you can sift the flour. Also, whole grains take more time to bake than white. Test for doneness with a toothpick or small knife inserted in the center (if it comes out dry and clean, the cake is done). It's better to have the outside a little too well done than half the middle under-cooked.

to being more nutritious than whole milk, is a natural sweet-ener; when you include it in a recipe, you can reduce other sweeteners.

THICKENERS

Many kinds of ingredients can be used as thickeners. Depending on the taste you want, you can add ground nuts, seeds, nut or seed butters, or wheat, barley, etc., flakes.

A NOTE ABOUT LEMONS

Lemons can be used to counteract the urge to eat sugar. They can also substitute for salt. Lemons should be used liberally.

Menus—Week Eight

Follow the menu guidelines from previous weeks; begin reinforcing changes from recent weeks. Continue greater use of poultry, fish, grains, and vegetables.

WEEK EIGHT

Recipes

EVERYTHING GOOD BIRTHDAY CAKE
YIELD: ONE 9-INCH CAKE

> *1½ cups whole wheat pastry flour*
> *1 teaspoon baking powder*
> *1 teaspoon baking soda*
> *1 teaspoon powdered nutmeg*
> *pinch of salt*
> *½ teaspoon allspice*
> *1 teaspoon cinnamon*
> *⅓ cup melted butter or oil*
> *½ cup fruit concentrate*
> *2 eggs, beaten*
> *½ cup unsweetened applesauce*

1. Preheat oven to 375 degrees.
2. Combine dry ingredients.
3. Combine liquid ingredients and add to dry. Mix well.
4. Pour mixture into a 9-inch cake pan and bake for 45 minutes or until inside is done. Allow to cool; add icing (see p. 190) if desired.

ICINGS FOR CAKES

Icings that don't use sugar sometimes present a real challenge. Here are some ideas.

Creamy Orange Icing
YIELD: 2 CUPS

> ½ cup butter
> ¾ cup honey
> ⅓ cup frozen orange juice concentrate (defrosted)
> ½ cup dry milk powder
> ½ cup slivered almonds

1. Cream butter and honey together.

2. Add orange juice concentrate; then add dry milk powder and mix until dissolved. Mix in almonds.

3. Spread evenly. Sprinkle with more almonds or carob chips. (The latter can be used to spell out a birthday message.)

Cashew-Fruit Icing
YIELD: 1½ CUPS

> 1 cup raw cashews
> ½ cup dates, figs, apricots, or a mixture
> 1 cup water
> 1 teaspoon vanilla extract

Place all ingredients in a blender or food processor and blend until smooth. Refrigerate until thickened. If mixture becomes too thick, add more water.

Carob-Amazake Frosting
YIELD: ¼ CUP

> 1 tablespoon arrowroot powder
> 1 cup Amazake (original flavor)

¼ carob chips (unsweetened)
¼ teaspoon vanilla extract

1. Dissolve arrowroot in Amazake. Place in pan over medium heat and bring to a boil, stirring continuously. Reduce heat and simmer for one hour, stirring occasionally.

2. Stir in carob chips and vanilla and simmer until carob has melted. Allow to cool before frosting cake.

Peanut Butter-Carob Glaze
Here's an icing you don't have to cook—great for snack attacks. You can even spread it on a rice cake.
YIELD: ¾ CUP

½ cup natural chunky peanut butter
2 tablespoons honey
½ teaspoon vanilla extract
1 teaspoon carob powder

Mix all ingredients well and spread on cake.

GOOD-FOR-YOU APPLE PIE
SERVES: 6

1 package Oronoque Orchards pie crust or your own
5 or 6 Granny Smith apples, peeled
1 teaspoon cinnamon
raisins, sliced peaches, sliced plums, juice-sweetened
jam (optional)

1. Preheat oven to 250 degrees.

2. Follow directions on package for baking bottom crust.

3. Slice apples and fill bottom crust. Sprinkle cinnamon on top and add raisins, etc., if you want variety or more sweetness.

4. Place top crust on, puncture in a few places, and bake for 20 minutes.

FRUIT POCKETS
YIELD: 4–6

Filling

>   1 large apple
>   2 tablespoons raisins
>   2 tablespoons chopped dates
>   2 tablespoons orange juice
>   2 teaspoons grated orange peel
>   ½ teaspoon arrowroot powder

Dough

>   1 cup whole wheat pastry flour
>   ¼ teaspoon salt
>   1½ teaspoons wheat germ
>   1½ teaspoons sesame seeds
>   6 tablespoons butter, margarine, or oil
>   2 tablespoons water

1. Peel and grate the apple. Add remaining filling ingredients (except for arrowroot) and mix well.

2. Cook over low heat and slowly stir in the arrowroot. Simmer, stirring continuously, until thickened. Remove from stove.

3. Combine flour, salt, wheat germ, and sesame seeds.

4. Cube butter (if using). Add butter, margarine, or oil and water to flour, and knead gently. Form into a ball. (Do not overknead as this will make pastry tough.)

5. Flatten dough with a rolling pin and then cut into squares.

6. Place a small amount of filling mixture in middle of squares, brush edges with water, and press together with a fork. Bake at 400 degrees for 20 minutes.

Variations: You can use your imagination to vary the fillings. Some ideas are other fruits in season such as pears, plums, peaches, or apricots; dried fruit; nuts. Because this pastry is not sweet, you can also use it as a pocket for vegetables, bean sprouts, etc.

GRAPE YOGURT JELLO
SERVES: 4

> 2 cups grape juice
> 1 package unflavored gelatin
> 1 container plain yogurt
> 2 teaspoons honey, maple syrup, or other natural
>   sweetener
> wheat germ or chopped nuts

1. Bring 1 cup of grape juice to a boil and mix in the gelatin.

2. Remove from heat, add the rest of the grape juice, and chill.

3. When gelatin has set, combine yogurt with honey and spread mixture on top. Sprinkle with wheat germ or chopped nuts.

Variation: Allow gelatin to set slightly, combine with yogurt and honey, and whip together; then chill until firm. This is more like a mousse. Other juices can be substituted for grape.

PUMPKIN OR SQUASH COOKIES
YIELD: 2 DOZEN SMALL COOKIES

There are many easy cookies you can make healthful by using ingredients such as whole wheat flour, oats, nut butter (peanut, sesame, almond, etc.), fresh or dried fruit, carob chips or powder, etc. This recipe is included because it uses an "important" vegetable in an unusual yet delicious way.

> *2 eggs*
> *1 cup honey or maple syrup*
> *½ cup melted butter, margarine, or oil*
> *1 tablespoon cinnamon*
> *1 tablespoon nutmeg*
> *½ teaspoon ground cloves*
> *½ teaspoon ground ginger*
> *2 teaspoons baking powder*
> *1½ cups whole wheat or rye flour*
> *¼ cup water*
> *2 cups cooked pumpkin or winter squash, mashed*

1. Preheat oven to 350 degrees.

2. Mix first 8 ingredients and then add flour, water, and vegetable.

3. Drop by spoonfuls onto lightly greased cookie sheet and bake until brown (about 15 minutes), but still moist inside. Remove from sheet immediately.

8

THE THIRD MONTH
AND BEYOND

Now that you are more familiar with the program, everyone in your family will be ready for the next step: making this program a way of life. The problem with most diet programs—whether they are like this one or designed for weight loss—is that once the initial goals are achieved, the tendency is to fall back into old habits. Eventually, the backslide is so extreme that you have to start all over again—in other words, "the yo-yo syndrome."

The authors are dedicated to preventing this from happening. You have spent valuable time and effort for the past two months in changing your child's eating habits. By now, you may already be seeing some good results in terms of scholastic and behavioral improvement. What a waste it would be to lose it all! Yet this is the time that is most critical in terms of reinforcing the changes. All the principles of this program have been set down. Now is the time for practice and finetuning.

It is also the time to take a look at some other important factors, namely the world outside. This includes:

- Care givers (baby-sitters and others)
- Friends, relatives, your child's peers and *their* parents
- Special events—holidays, birthday parties, etc.
- Eating out and take-out, especially in fast-food restaurants
- School lunch: eating school lunches or brown bagging lunches—and what to do in either case.

Practice and Fine-Tuning

Now that everything is aboveboard and not sneaky, your child can get more involved with the planning and preparation of his meals. Most children will welcome some kind of participation; this can take several forms.

MENU PLANNING

Based on the food diary and other indicators of what he liked or disliked, your child can help plan menus. You may not want to do this for every day; in fact, you can use it as a negotiating point by trading off meals you want him to have for ones that are his favorites. Menus could be designed and posted in the kitchen. An interesting idea is to have one day a week that is "child's choice." Your child would plan all the meals for that day and even help with the shopping and preparation. Or, you might have "child's breakfast weekend," during which the child plans and prepares breakfasts for the entire weekend.

SHOPPING

Some children love to shop for groceries. If your child is old enough to do it, this is an excellent opportunity for him to take responsibility for his food. Even if you must accompany a child on a shopping trip, you can still allow him autonomy once there. There is no better place to learn all about label reading than in a store. Children get a firsthand education about what really goes into food.

COMMUNAL MEALS

If you embarked on the Eating for A's Program with others (neighbors, relatives, friends) you might want to celebrate your progress by having some communal meals. Each family could prepare a dish and eat the meal together. This could be a festive occasion, in addition to being both time- and energy-efficient. Even if you were the sole participant in the program, you might want to have a communal meal (using your recipe ideas) as a way of introducing others to the program and alleviating any feelings of being an outsider that your child may have.

FAMILY COOKBOOK

Again, using food diaries and family likes and dislikes as a basis, everyone could participate in producing a cookbook of favorite recipes with weekly menus that can be used as a reference by everyone.

FRUIT, VEGETABLE, AND GRAIN OF THE WEEK

To keep things lively and to keep everyone from getting bored, you might introduce the idea of a fruit, etc., of the week. This could either be something no one has ever eaten, something just in season, or a particular favorite chosen for that week. The choice should be left entirely to your child. You might then plan meals together featuring these foods. It need not be one of each of the above; it could be two vegetables, two fruits, etc. The point is to keep increasing the consumption of vital learning-enhancing foods.

Care Givers

Baby-sitters, relatives, or others are going to be with your child while you're away. The best way to insure that your child is getting the right food is to have it prepared in advance. Then you can just give instructions as to how and when to serve it. Next best is elaborate instructions. It may be necessary to have a discussion or, even better, write down some of the "rules"—post them, if necessary. Make it clear that care givers cannot make any exceptions, and do this when your child is present, so there won't be any manipulating behind your back. Be careful to include the child—show that it's a mutual rule (even if you're still not sure it is and are meeting with resistance!).

Grandparents and other doting relatives present a particular challenge. They are usually quite indulgent and leave the disciplining to the parents. In this enviable role, they do a lot of treating, and the treats are often "sweets." They might not consider snacks "food," and won't even think to mention which ones your child ate. Before you come down too hard on grandparents, remember that they grew up in a more innocent time. If they protest that "a few sweets can't hurt," you may need to explain to them that there are far more junk foods and questionable additives on the market now than when they were young. You can show them some of the facts in this book—namely, that American children have never been in worse shape, and the contributing causes are life-style and diet. Of course, you may need to practice your diplomatic skills. Explain, as neutrally as possible, why your child is on this program and what the boundaries are. In all likelihood, regardless of what they really think, relatives will comply.

School Lunch

Eating in school is the type of eating out your child does most frequently, and it is no simple matter to deal with it. The question is, "How much control do I have?" Obviously, you have more control if you give your child a lunch to take; and seemingly none if he eats the school lunch. But is this true?

THE CAFETERIA

If your child goes to one of those rare schools that has a truly nutrition-conscious food program, you are extremely fortunate and he will have a relatively easy time following this diet. But, in all probability, his school is not like this. Although you may not choose to get involved in changing the program, there are a few things you should do to help improve it.

RESTRICTING THE SALE OF "COMPETITIVE" FOOD

One of the worst deterrents to nutritious eating in school is the availability of sodas, candy, potato chips, etc., in vending machines or snack stands. This was dramatically illustrated in the Bogalusa Heart Study—the most extensive investigation of its kind ever done anywhere. Over a period of 15 years, 10,000 people in Bogalusa, Louisiana, participated in a study to investigate the causes of cardiac problems. More than 80 percent of the schoolchildren there participated. Investigators discovered that at least two-thirds of these children were getting too much sodium, fat, and sugar, making them seriously at risk for heart problems in adulthood. The school lunches were contributing greatly to this imbalance.

In terms of competitive foods, the Bogalusa Junior High School opened its snack stand just to make money to buy school supplies. Within *one minute*, they made 60 transactions: four kinds of candy, soda pop, five kinds of potato chips, tortilla chips, Cheez Doodles, and so on—mostly fat, salt, and sugar: a nutritionist's nightmare.

Every effort should be made to restrict these sales and to remove all nonnutritious items from vending machines. Parents can have an effective voice against these sales. Vending machines and snack stands can sell nutritious items such as fresh fruit, unsalted popcorn, and fruit juice. You can be supported by the fact that there are many precedents for this action: in fact, some state legislatures and municipal councils have passed laws forbidding the sale of junk food in the schools, as in Los Angeles.

CANDY SALES

It's necessary to mention the very touchy subject of fundraising. All schools encourage parents and others to get involved in fundraising for worthy projects such as the baseball team's uniforms. Unfortunately, the funds are usually raised through the sale of candy. Now that you've become your child's (and hopefully, all children's) advocate for good nutrition, this will probably seem hypocritical to you. It is an issue being debated in many schools throughout the country and in some cases, it has been handled by selling such items as T-shirts, books, video and audio cassettes or having spelling bees, flea markets, and auctions—in short, getting food out of fundraising.

For more information on school lunches, see questions and answers in Chapter 11, pp. 243–45.

BROWN BAG LUNCHES

You will probably be supplying your child with his lunch at school. The same principles apply to brown bagging as to other meals: balance, variety, good nutrition, and taste.

Some suggestions for brown bag lunches can be found in Chapter 6, Week Two. Here are additional ones.

Sandwiches: Whole grain bread should be used exclusively but can be cut into interesting shapes (use a cookie cutter) and filled with any variety of foods you can think of—including leftover meat loaf, fish, chicken, etc. Try using the vast array of nut butters found in natural food stores (pistachio, cashew, almond, to name a few). Dot pieces of dried fruit or raw vegetables on cream cheese (or tofu "cream cheese") fillings.

Pack all the fixings for sandwiches in separate containers and let your child assemble it himself. This will not only be something different but also prevent sandwiches from getting soggy. Another tip for preventing sogginess: spread butter or margarine to the edges of each slice of bread, then fill with something freezable (not cheese, hard-cooked eggs, mayonnaise, or raw vegetables). Wrap well and freeze for up to two weeks. Pack the sandwiches frozen in the lunchbox; they will defrost completely in 2 to 3 hours.

Non-sandwiches: Who says you have to have a sandwich every day? Pack yogurt (without sugar, of course), or vegetable or fruit salad in containers; instead of bread, include bran or carrot muffins or corn chips; or try hard-boiled eggs, cut in half with the yolk scooped out and filled with tuna salad (for a change); stuff tomatoes or avocados with chicken, tuna, or egg salad; serve chunks of cheese and whole fruit; or chicken or turkey legs or wings.

Hot stuff: A wide-mouthed thermos is a wonderful addition to the lunch box. You can fill it with delicious soups, macaroni and cheese, spaghetti and meatballs, brown rice or other grains and vegetables, or anything else you want to serve hot. You don't need additional plates because everything can be eaten directly out of the wide-mouthed thermos. (You can even "cook" soup while your child is in class: in the morning, just cut up vegetables and put them into the thermos with hot water and seasonings. By lunchtime, your child will have soup.)

Drinks can be prepared in a wide-mouthed thermos as well as in a regular one. Include hot carob, hot apple cider, or herb teas in your child's lunch box.

Cold stuff: Using the wide-mouthed thermos, you can serve cold sesame noodles, taboule, cold rice salad, or guacamole; for drinks, you can pack frozen individual fruit juice containers, which incidentally will also serve to keep the rest of the food cold.

Desserts: Fresh fruit is a natural, but you may also want to include some nutritious cake or cookie, a baked apple, Kanten (p. 131), or Brown Rice Pudding (p. 142). Desserts may count for more in brown bag lunches than at any other time because of all the potential peer pressure. You don't want your child to feel like he is an outsider because his lunch isn't at all like his friends' lunches.

With such delicious fare, you might think your child couldn't wait to eat his bag lunch. But it's not so simple. There are other children also eating bag lunches and, though theirs are probably not nearly as nutritious, they may be more interesting to him. It is common for children to swap food items with friends, and the last thing you want is for your child to trade his apple for a Yankee Doodle. You cannot control this completely because you're not there, but you must be as firm as possible about the rules. You can do your own swapping. For example, when he comes home, if he hasn't eaten the Yankee Doodle, you can swap it for another healthier food he prefers. Use your ingenuity to the fullest; it's really important to win this one.

An older child might be schooled to actually turn lunch into a nutrition lesson. When tempted by a friend's junk food snack, he might read off the ingredients to anyone listening and then refuse it. But don't count on this kind of compliance!

Eating Out

RESTAURANTS

On the Eating for A's Program, restaurant dining can be a challenging but not an insurmountable experience. What should be an enjoyable excursion may turn into a verbal boxing match.

The trick for successful eating out is not to be intractable. Probably no restaurant (even those calling themselves "natural") will meet the standards of your kitchen. But then, why go to a restaurant to eat the same food you eat at home? It's fun to eat something different, but you don't have to sacrifice all your nutritional gains to do so. Here are some tips:

- Order meat, fish, and poultry dishes broiled or baked, not fried or deep-fried.
- Avoid heavy sauces.
- Avoid items that may contain artificial additives, sugar, etc., such as salad dressings, hot sauce.
- Inquire if vegetables are fresh (not canned) and only order fresh or frozen ones.
- Avoid desserts with sugar. Instead order fresh fruit or melon.

Above all, do this with grace and good nature; there's nothing so guaranteed to make everyone uncomfortable as a person who is fanatical in giving orders for food.

FAST-FOOD RESTAURANTS

Like it or not, you will probably be eating out most frequently in fast-food restaurants. These are in a category all by themselves because the foods they serve are notoriously high in fat, salt, and sugar. Fast-food establishments are under no obligation to disclose the ingredients in the food, and this can present a major problem for someone on this program—or in fact, on any special diet program. *The Fast-Food Guide* (see References) is a book that is a must for anyone who eats in a fast-food establishment. It charts all the major fast-food restaurants with particulars on everything they serve.

The following information and tips have been culled from this book:

- **Sugar:** Fast-food manufacturers add sugar, corn syrup, etc., to many foods. For instance:
  French fries are coated with sugar so that they will brown when they hit the hot grease.
  Batter coating contains a lot of sugar.
  Colas, soft drinks, juice drinks, and milkshakes contain a great deal of sugar; the latter often contains no milk. Order pure juice, milk, or water instead.
- **Fat:** It's hard to escape high fat content in the popular fast food dishes. But here are some tips:
  Avoid mayonnaise, tartar sauce, dressings such as Thousand Island, blue cheese.
  Avoid cheeseburgers: one slice of cheese adds more than 100 calories to McDonald's Quarter Pounder. (Besides, the cheese probably has artificial colorings and is high in sodium.)
  Avoid anything that is called "whopper," "deluxe," "super," or anything else that sounds big. These are the most caloric

and the most expensive. Do not order extra cheese on pizzas; if you want anything extra get vegetables. Forget bacon.

Order roast beef instead of hamburger: the fattiest roast beef is leaner than the leanest hamburger.

Fish and chicken: Although throughout this program, we have recommended increasing the consumption of fish and poultry, this doesn't necessarily hold true in fast-food restaurants. Be careful of fish and chicken that is breaded, particularly "extra crispy." Some establishments, however, such as Arby's, Arthur Treacher's, and D'Lites offer baked or broiled fish and chicken.

■ *Salt:* There's hidden (and not-so-hidden) salt in almost every fast-food item. All you can do is try to hold the line on pickles, mustard, relish, catsup, hot sauce, and barbecue sauce.

Avoid processed meats such as frankfurters, bacon, ham, and sausages; on pizzas, avoid pepperoni, anchovies, salami, and olives.

A Few Final Tips:

Avoid special kid's meal packs; you're paying extra for the packaging.

Take advantage of salad bars. Many fast-food establishments are constantly improving their menus with the addition of fresh vegetables, baked potatoes, etc. At the very least, order a hamburger with lettuce and tomato; this may be the best "deal" you can make with a child who insists on eating in one of these restaurants.

OTHER PEOPLE'S HOMES

In a sense this form of eating out challenges the program the most. For one thing, when your child is invited to some-

206 Eating for A's

one's home for a party or dinner, it is impolite to spout off a long laundry list of "no-no's." If the hostess is a close friend or relative, you may be able to ask for certain things. But in general, you will probably just have to let go—after all, this program should not be perceived as one big sacrifice of either yours or your child's social life.

The best way to handle these situations is to prepare in advance. Make sure your child gets plenty of good food before he goes to the party. If he is satisfied, he will probably not fill up on junk. If he does, don't panic. These are extraordinary circumstances and you cannot afford to be rigid. Besides, there is a strong possibility that because he has been eating so healthfully, his body will react to the onslaught of poor food and he may get a stomach ache or a headache—which will prove to be a far better teacher than you could ever be!

Holidays and Special Occasions

BIRTHDAY PARTIES

During the time your child has been on this program, you've been revising a lot of rules and customs. Where is it written in stone that a birthday party is an arena to pig out on junk? Why are sugary cake, soda, and candy the main attractions? You cannot afford to be hypocritical or give mixed messages. The whole family has (hopefully) conformed to certain standards for eating well, and they cannot be compromised at a joyous event, such as a birthday party. In fact, because it's a celebration, it will require more careful attention. If you give the message that when we're celebrating, when we're having a good time, it's all right to eat foods we don't ordinarily, then you are setting up a judgment that the day-to-day more nutritious foods are dull and boring, whereas nonnutritious foods are really "fun." It's the wrong message and one that will hinder the progress of your child and make it harder for this program to become a way of life.

Now, this doesn't mean that a birthday party can't be fun. On the contrary, what makes most birthday parties memorable are the games, entertainment, and the decorations (why not have a beautiful vegetable or fruit centerpiece, for a change?). Food is part of a party, but it need not be the most important part. It should be there and it should be delicious but it must be consistent with your philosophy. Furthermore, children invariably return from birthday parties filled to the brim with junk and are unable or unwilling to eat anything decent. Why not turn the birthday party into a wonderful feast full of delicious but also nutritious food? This need not entail extra work, and kids will not be the only ones to enjoy it; their parents will be very appreciative too.

The kind of birthday party that makes sense and will also be unique is one that is actually a meal, such as a brunch, lunch, or early dinner. Children can be served cafeteria-style. Place items on a long table or bench and have guests make their own sandwiches and salads. You can even have bowls of dried fruits, nuts, maple syrup, and yogurt so they can make their own sundaes for dessert. Younger children can make rice cake "faces" spread with peanut butter, cream cheese, with pieces of vegetable, fruit, and raisins for eyes, nose, etc., and then place an individual birthday candle on each.

The same goes for drinks: You can lay out all the raw materials such as low-fat milk, carob syrup, plain soda, fruit juice, or syrup from fruit extract, "good" ice cream, etc. Last of all, the obligatory birthday cake can be home-baked from the most nutritious ingredients (see p. 189 for a sample recipe).

HALLOWEEN

This occasion deserves a heading of its own for having the dubious distinction of topping the list of junk-food nightmares. Parents and teachers alike concur that after Halloween, kids "act out" the most. If you're fortunate enough to control *where* your child "tricks or treats," he may come back with a bag filled with raisins and nuts. But chances are he'll bring in a year's worth of junk food, and you'll have to deal with what he hasn't already eaten (not much, if you're lucky).

One parent we know survived many Halloweens and brought up three healthy, nutrition-conscious girls with this tradeoff: The girls would dump their bag of goodies on the table when they came home, and the mother would decide what they could keep. She would replace every item they had to discard with something acceptable—either a nutritious snack or a toy, etc. It worked so well that she successfully "traded" after birthday parties and other occasions too.

OTHER CELEBRATIONS

Holiday dinners are different from birthday parties in that other adults are present. Yet this is no reason to "fall off the program." We were once present at a holiday dinner party where the hostess' daughter, aged nine, was taking the celery sticks from a platter of raw vegetables and eating them like candy. In some amazement, we asked our friend why she was eating them with such enthusiasm. "We always serve sliced raw vegetables at celebrations," she said. Her daughter associated that food with having a fun time, so she joyously dived into the celery.

Your biggest problem at holiday dinners may be the adults. It is wise to explain beforehand some of the details and benefits of the Eating For A's Program. Make sure to stress that *the whole family* is on it, so that your child will not be treated in any special fashion. The fact that you, as an adult, are also involved may keep others from making disparaging comments or displaying negative attitudes about the food. They may even turn out to enjoy it so much that there are a few new "converts"! At the very least, it can be a festive occasion, unmarked by upsets over food.

9

BREAKING THE BARRIERS

Most people familiar with sports know the name Roger Bannister. But on May 6, 1954, it was a name that echoed around the world like a thunderclap. Everyone was suddenly aware of new human possibilities after Roger Bannister—at the age of 25—became the first human being to run the mile in less than four minutes. He had broken a barrier that was once considered physically impossible.

Ever since that momentous occasion, Roger Bannister has been studying athletic excellence. Knighted and now dean of the Department of Neurophysiology at Oxford University, Sir Roger recently shared a secret with another miler, an American named Joe Falcon. Observing Falcon at the famous Penn Relays, Bannister could tell that while the American had great potential, something was slowing him down. The two men met for a short time and discussed training and diet habits. Bannister gave Falcon some simple advice which significantly improved his athletic performance.

"He told me about a study showing that carbonated beverages decrease the blood's oxygen-carrying capacity," Falcon recalled. The study illustrated that carbon gas in sodas like Coke and Pepsi competed against oxygen for space in the bloodstream. This made it more difficult to supply oxygen-starved muscles during exercise.

Up until his meeting with Bannister, Joe was a four-Coke-a-day man. But when he eliminated the sodas, his recovery after an exhaustive workout doubled and his breathing level dropped within the first minute. Simply eliminating sodas from his diet, he alleged, allowed him to work harder, train more aggressively, and recover more quickly.

Three months after his meeting with Bannister and eliminating sodas, Joe Falcon managed to beat the world's best milers in three consecutive televised races: The Bislet Games in Oslo, Norway, The Good Will Games in Seattle, Washington, and the New York Games in New York City, *all in the same month!* His Oslo mile time was a phenomenal 3 minutes and 49.31 seconds, *within a second and a half of the existing world record!*

Although your child isn't training to break a world track record, he's probably drinking sodas in a way that is self-damaging. American adolescents now consume an average of over 1,000 cans of soda per year. That's close to 3 cans a day for every teenager in America. Americans already consume more sodas than water, and more than three times as much soda as both cow's milk and fruit juices combined!

Of course, parents might feel that it's easy for an elite athlete to break physical barriers through a diet change, but their child is just average—so what difference does one or two sodas a day make?

The answer is: a world of difference.

Soda—the Liquid Candy Bar

In consuming sodas, American children are drinking nothing more than liquid candy bars with fizz. And American children have never been in worse physical shape.

Consider this:

- 40 percent of children between the ages of 6 and 17 cannot do a single pull-up.
- In the 50-yard dash, the girls of today are significantly slower than those tested 10 years ago.
- Only one state, Illinois, still requires the daily exercise for children that President Kennedy had proposed 25 years ago. (And these exercise programs were developed because children were considered unfit then!)
- Fifteen years ago, the American Cancer Society found that obese people were much more likely to suffer from cancer of the uterus, gallbladder, kidney, stomach, colon, and breast than nonobese people. And yet, in the past 15 years, obesity among our kids has actually risen by 40 percent. A major contributing factor is soft drinks.

But how can parents change their children's attitudes toward sodas? The combination of caffeine and sugar is among the most habit forming in the world—colas contain both. And the soft drink companies spend $400 million yearly to advertise skinny, wonderful, healthy, active kids drinking sodas, persuading your child that he can be like them.

The only way you can make this image of a healthy, active child real is to *keep all commercial sodas out of the house.* Healthier sodas can be made with fruit juice and seltzer (which is carbonated water), the recipes for which are on p. 105. You can use the anecdote about Joe Falcon to show your children what sodas can do—quite the reverse of the TV ads.

And if your child really wants to feel as good as the children drinking sodas on the screen seem to, instill within him a commitment to exercise. Exercise is a superb way of strengthening your child's self-esteem, and will lead him naturally toward choosing foods that reinforce a healthy image.

Exercise and Self-Esteem

Here is a dramatic illustration of this fact. In 1973, Alexander Schauss was a probation parole officer in Albuquerque, New Mexico. According to FBI statistics, Albuquerque had the highest felony crime rate in the United States, and the second highest per capita rate of heroin addiction. He was approached to form a track team composed of poor underprivileged girls who lived in "El Barrio"—the ghetto—and other parts of the community. These were children who were in trouble at school and with the local police, or needed a structured activity. They came from broken homes; some of their parents were drug addicts, alcoholics, and prostitutes.

Initially, the track team was formed as a means of giving the children a constructive activity after school. Schauss had hoped to prove that underprivileged youngsters could compete as effectively as affluent children if they had proper training and nutrition.

Unfortunately, in their first race his team placed dead last—in fact, they were not even *close* to the other runners at the finish line. The girls were ridiculed by other children for their performance and their appearance. Because they were poor, none of them had money for uniforms like the other teams. At the end of the race, their worst fears had come true. They sat down in the bleachers, some of them crying with shame, because they had proved to themselves and the world at large that they would always remain second-class citizens:

without talent, self-discipline, or the ability to achieve—
forever wearing hand-me-down clothes from older brothers
and sisters, who were models of angry despair.

Yet Schauss found a way of inspiring these children. He
convinced them that if they trained with him, listened to his
advice, and obeyed his rules they had a chance at becoming
track champions. By winning their confidence, he won their
obedience, and they immediately began to concentrate on
training. Part of his program included supplementation with
vitamin C, nutritious morning breakfasts, and *a total avoidance of all soft drinks and candy snacks.* As their bodies grew
stronger, and they learned to discipline their free time, their
school marks improved. As they achieved more in school,
their confidence in their abilities deepened.

During the summer of 1974, Schauss trained his team
while all the other track and field competitors vacationed. In
the fall, their training efforts paid off handsomely. *The team
won every AAU track meet for children of their age group* that it
entered, and this included winning numerous regional cham-
pionships and setting AAU indoor track records later that
winter.

A number of the students went on to attend college on
athletic scholarships, and one of them won an award from
Sports Illustrated magazine for breaking *six* age-group records
in one weekend, in two separate states, at meets held at
5,500- and 6,200-foot elevations. (The extra vitamin C and
vitamin E helped the girls adjust better to the rarefied al-
titudes.)

Both Joe Falcon, and the girls' team of Albuquerque, New
Mexico, had in common an *awareness* of the deeper levels of
their being—levels that were nourished by the body *and* the
spirit. Throughout this book, the authors have put together a
program based on research and personal experience. It is a
scientific program that calculates the energy contained in

certain foods needed by the body and selects specific nutrients to nurture the brain. But there is something that can't be measured in the Eating for A's Program: the effect of the right food on the body's inner strengths: courage, determination, and willpower. These inner strengths become energized—especially in children—through cardiovascular fitness.

TV, Cholesterol, and Fitness

The question most often put to researchers like Alexander Schauss is: "What would be the *single* most important change you'd recommend to improve our children's health?" His advice is always: "a healthy nurturing diet *combined* with physical fitness through regular exercise." It's the kind of advice that no one disagrees with because everyone's heard it before, but how many parents apply it to their own children?

How many hours does *your* child exercise a week? How does this compare with the hours spent sitting in front of the television? The average child watches more than 25 hours per week. Television viewing is taking the place of exercise, adding to already sedentary life-styles. At the same time that children are watching commercials for junk foods, many of them are nibbling at the very foods portrayed on the screen. It gives them a strong feeling of *belonging* to what they're watching, of being *an intimate part* of the program.

An ongoing study at the University of California–Irvine has been examining the relationship between children's TV viewing and their cholesterol levels. In a review of these kinds of studies, the American Academy of Pediatrics considers any serum cholesterol level above 175 serious enough to warrant diet therapy for children over two years old. The University of California study has found that children who watch TV from two to four hours a day are *50 percent* more likely to have an elevated serum cholesterol level than children who watch less TV.

The California study also revealed that 24 percent of the children examined had serum cholesterol levels above those considered safe by the American Academy of Pediatrics. In 8 percent the cholesterol count was above 200, a level considered to merit medical attention.

In short, watching more than two hours of TV a day endangers a child's health—primarily because of the lack of exercise.

Kinds of Exercise

Exercise is simply a *sustained* activity level for the heart. It does not have to be an organized sport, but it does have to work the heart well above the level experienced at rest. And the benefits of exercise can be realized at any age—for senior citizens or preschoolers.

For example, Miami Medical School's Childhood Development Center conducted a study of 24 preschoolers for 8 weeks. Half the children were allowed to play with their friends in "free play" in the school playground. Essentially, they were allowed to do anything they wanted. The other half were enrolled in a daily thirty-minute program of aerobic exercises. At the end of eight weeks, the children were tested. Those children who had engaged in the aerobic exercise program showed significant gains in *self-esteem, agility, and cardiovascular fitness,* as compared to their schoolmates who were just "playing" in the playground.

This study and many others suggest that being satisfied that our children are out "playing" is not enough. *What kind of play* are they involved in? We can't assume they'll naturally get exercise, whatever they're doing.

ONGOING EXERCISE PROGRAMS

Studies by the National Center for Health Statistics estimates that if America's couch potatoes were to exercise as little as 20 minutes three times a week, at least 22,000 lives a year could be saved from heart disease alone.

Therefore, if your child is not part of an ongoing exercise program, the Eating for A's prescription would be to enroll him in one after school. Karate, gymnastics, soccer, swimming, basketball, track—any sport, in fact, which requires a sustained activity well above that experienced at rest. The longer the level of exercise is maintained, the greater the benefits to cardiovascular health. In fact, exercise might be something the whole family would enjoy doing together.

MUSICAL STAIRS

People often use the weather, appointments, all sorts of excuses to avoid exercise, when with a little ingenuity they can find ways to exercise right at hand. Alexander Schauss was visiting the remote town of Bethel, Alaska, years ago to give a lecture. The outside temperature was 45 degrees below zero—too cold for anything but staying inside to keep warm, so the family used a simple set of stairs to their loft as a fun place for daily exercise. Each family member chose some favorite records to be played on their record player, and then the whole family marched up and down to the music.

It seemed like so much fun that he soon joined in, selecting an old hit from the Fifties that had the kids rolling on the floor in hysteria. Thirty minutes later, not only had everyone gotten in a good aerobic workout, but the family had had a lot of fun doing it.

SEGMENT TRAINING

Parents who exercise regularly are far more apt to have children who grow up exercising. Such parents know that the local health club usually offers after-school programs that develop children's cardiovascular endurance. By periodically testing children's bodily measurements and physical abilities, these clubs can offer constant feedback on a child's progress. The results of such tests often motivate children to try harder and support their self-confidence when they do.

But what about the family that simply doesn't have time to exercise regularly? Alexander Schauss recommends "segment training" as a means to accommodate a busy schedule. One of the misconceptions we have about exercising is that it has to be done all at one time each day. For many people this is impractical. If training is broken up into 10- or 15-minute segments, however, the results can be just as beneficial.

This is true not only for children but also for adults. A 1990 paper in the *American Journal of Cardiology* confirmed that segment training produced excellent results. In the study 18 healthy men completed 30 minutes of exercise training per day. Of this group, 9 men exercised for a full half hour; for the other 9, the exercise program was divided into three 10-minute bouts of daily exercise, separated by at least 4 hours. After 8 weeks, both groups of men improved their oxygen carrying capacity and training intensity. However, adherence to the unsupervised exercise training program was highest in the short duration group, which completed 93 percent of the prescribed exercise periods. The authors concluded that for many individuals, "short bouts of exercise may fit better into a busy schedule."

Exercise and Attitude

Perhaps the most important contribution regular exercise makes to children is a positive mental attitude. Conditioning their bodies produces immediate and long-term benefits in their mood, self-image, and general sense of well-being. This in turn motivates children to do better and try harder at solving problems. In addition, exercise diminishes five of the eight risk factors of heart disease: obesity, stress, hypertension, high cholesterol, and sedentary life-style.

Exercise and Muscles

Regular exercise is also the only way known to work muscles, and muscles produce movement of the body, which benefits both the child's appearance and overall fitness. As a child's muscles increase in size and strength, his bodily movements become more secure and efficient. Muscles also protect the body from harm by allowing it to move quickly to avoid danger and injury. Strengthened muscles also result in indirect benefits to tendons, ligaments, and bones, which strengthen the entire skeleton.

One of the reasons the Eating For A's Program emphasizes the nutrient chromium is that it is intimately involved in the development of muscle mass through its contribution to insulin, which also regulates fat metabolism. Recent studies have shown that individuals consuming adequate levels of chromium lose excess body fat while gaining muscle mass, *if exercising*. Without exercise, this benefit is not seen.

Effect of Exercise on Bone Density, Circulation, and Respiratory System

In addition, exercise helps maintain *bone density* in children because it stimulates the uptake of calcium, magnesium, and other essential nutrients into the bone.

Exercise also helps combat allergies because it improves the circulation. An improved circulatory system helps carry away the waste products that accumulate in the body's tissues. It also strengthens the respiratory system and stimulates the mucous lining when inhalant allergies attack. As the mucous lining becomes more moist, the antibodies in the lining become more active, which promotes resistance to the infection.

If Your Child Is Not Exercising . . .

If your child is not interested in physical fitness, the first step is to examine your own attitude toward exercise. The overweight parent, and those who smoke, are generally the least likely to maintain a regular exercise schedule. However, even these parents entering into a contract to exercise over an initial 12-week-period make noticeable improvements physically if they exercise three days a week.

Roberta: A Case History

Eleven-year-old Roberta was asked to visit Alexander Schauss with her parents because of her explosive behavior. She had already been placed in a "contained" special education environment which provided three teachers for every 12 students. After the school's psychologist and counselor had evaluated Roberta, Schauss was asked if he could find any physiological causes for her classroom outbursts.

Like her parents, Roberta was obese. She weighed thirty pounds above her ideal weight range. During the interview, she was terribly serious, and no matter how hard Schauss tried, he could not bring a smile to her face. They talked about her favorite TV shows, comic books, and friends, when all of a sudden she declared, "I'm hungry—can I go?"

"What are you hungry for?" he asked.

"Potato chips."

"And that's enough?" he said. "That's all?"

"Yes," she said.

After half an hour, it became apparent that Roberta not only ate poorly but was also constantly criticized for her weight by her parents, who were also noticeably overweight and out of shape. After meeting with the parents, Schauss concluded that parental support was totally lacking in her life. They never praised Roberta or served as proper models so that Roberta might see herself as a worthwhile human being.

"Overweight children stand a much better chance of slimming down if their overweight parents reduce as well," Schauss advised. Like Roberta, they were asked to make a commitment to a diet change, supporting their child's efforts through praise every step of the way. The parents had themselves been fat when young, and *their* parents had also constantly criticized them for their weight. It was time to break this negative cycle, and the parents agreed to cooperate.

In addition, it was stressed that Roberta should participate in some physical activity after school. Because she had a negative self-image, Roberta didn't want to. She was ashamed of the way she looked and afraid other children would make fun of her. The solution was to draw up an *exercise contract*.

Roberta and her parents sat down and agreed on:

222 Eating for A's

1. What was acceptable exercise.
2. What the parents had to do so that Roberta would agree to a 2-month trial period.

Roberta agreed to an exercise program if her parents would take out the garbage in her place. She didn't want to do it anymore and she particularly wanted her parents to take it on—because in Roberta's eyes, they would look foolish doing that task. If they were willing to look foolish to her, then she was willing to look foolish to others.

The exercise contract worked very well. Roberta had seen a number of seemingly "fat" female swimmers who were more powerful than the boys in the water. Their figures were not really fat, just roundly muscular, and when they swam in the water, they moved beautifully.

Roberta began swimming after school and was eventually invited to train with the swimming team. In time, the school reported a definite improvement in Roberta's behavior. She began to relax, joke around with the other students, and socialize more freely. Her self-esteem improved, even though she remained somewhat overweight. Swimming allowed her to discover something she'd always dreamed of: a sense that she wasn't ugly and sometimes was perhaps even beautiful.

Your Attitude Toward Exercise

If your child isn't exercising and just comes home to watch television, the first step is to assess your own attitude. Stanford University developed an exercise attitude questionnaire some years ago that helps reveal your respect for your body. This self-assessment attitude test encourages a discussion about exercise. For example, statement # 1 says: "Exercise makes a person feel better." If you agree, then you should ask yourself why you aren't exercising.

This kind of self-testing not only allowed Roberta's parents to assess their own attitudes toward exercise but also the reasons for these attitudes.

Exercise Attitudes Test

1. Exercise makes a person feel better.
2. It is hard for me to stick to a regular schedule of physical activity.
3. People who don't exercise are more likely to get sick.
4. I usually drive or ride short distances rather than walk.
5. It is hard for me to find time to exercise on a regular basis.
6. When I exercise or play sports, I feel self-conscious about the way I look to others.
7. Exercise helps reduce stress.
8. Exercise helps a person's appearance.
9. I think I get enough exercise.
10. Exercise is really only important for athletes.
11. For the most part, exercise programs are boring.
12. People who exercise regularly are less likely to get a heart attack.

The questions in this attitude test help anticipate the reasons you may have for not signing a contract with your child. Yes, exercise *can be boring.* If this is going to be an excuse to drop out of your commitment, then make sure you don't select an exercise program that's boring from the start. If your choices of an existing program are discussed and weighed prior to the written contract, you have every chance of succeeding in the end.

As your child becomes more involved with sports (unless he is already) you might want to give him the benefit of superior training through sports nutrition, which follows in the next chapter.

10

Sports Nutrition

Children always enjoy enhancing their athletic abilities but rarely think of food as their energy source. When they do think about food, it's usually the wrong kind. The information in this chapter will enable you to enhance your child's athletic performance through sports nutrition.

For the competitive child athlete, fatigue is the common enemy. Whatever his arena—gym, swimming pool, court, playing field, or track—his training and development require building energy and stamina. Since the first scientific studies were conducted 100 years ago, a great deal has been learned about energy and fatigue.

Carbohydrates and Exercise

The most desirable source of food energy comes from carbohydrates, comprised of sugars, starches, and indigestible fibrous materials called fiber. Carbohydrates can be broken down into two categories: simple and complex. Sucrose (sugar), honey, fresh and dried fruit, jams and jellies, fruit juices and fruit drinks are the most common sources of simple carbohydrates. Complex carbohydrates are found mostly in grains (breads, pasta, rice, etc.) and certain vegetables such as potatoes, carrots, and other root vegetables.

The difference between simple and complex carbohydrates can be explained in terms of the simplest sugar that our bodies use for energy: *glucose*. Simple carbohydrates have only one or two molecules of glucose linked together, whereas complex carbohydrates consist of many links. Enzymes in the digestive tract break up these links, releasing the individual molecules of glucose for use by the body. Because complex carbohydrates have many more links to break down, it takes more time to break up all the glucose molecules. Therefore, complex carbohydrates represent a *slow-release source of energy*. Rather than getting overwhelmed with sudden increases in glucose energy (which happens in the extreme when consuming white sugar), cells are given moderate and steady amounts, which provide consistent levels of energy. Consistent energy is the best way to fuel the rapid motor nerve firings of the mind and heart during exercise.

Complex carbohydrates should account for a large proportion of your child's diet. Major health organizations are recommending that any healthy diet contain a minimum of *55 percent carbohydrates*, with the remaining caloric-sources coming from *less than 30 percent fats*, and *less than 15 percent proteins*. A rapidly mounting body of evidence indicates that fat intake well below 30 percent of total calories is advisable, that an intake of about 20 percent may actually be optimal.

Therefore, a diet rich in complex carbohydrates, most experts agree, is the best one for training and competitive performance, and for delaying the onset of the muscle's growing exhaustion, or "muscle fatigue." Starch, as we mentioned, is a carbohydrate. Many people mistakenly believe that starches are fattening and will avoid foods like potatoes and the other foods mentioned above. But, at four calories per gram, carbohydrates are not fattening. It's the butter, sour cream, cheese, and other trimmings that add to the caloric value of these foods. However, if a child overindulges in simple carbohydrates, such as white table sugar, the level of *glucose* (blood sugar) that is not used for energy will be converted to and stored as fat.

How to Prevent Muscle Fatigue

It was always believed that muscles worked during exercise because the central nervous system sent messages through the motor nerves initiating the muscles' contraction. When fatigue set in, scientists found the rate of motor nerve firings decreased sharply. More recently, scientists discovered that the causes of exercise-induced muscle fatigue are more complicated.

The question scientists asked was: How does the body prevent the self-destructive action of a muscular "overloading" (or self-damage) during exercise? Potassium, it was discovered, was one of the key nutrients that protected the muscle cell. The loss of potassium in the cells of the muscle affect the rate of muscle contraction. Therefore, no matter how hard your child tries to keep going, the loss of potassium inevitably will exhaust him. If this didn't happen, continued muscular activity would result in serious muscular damage. By ensuring that there is an ample supply of potassium in the bloodstream during exercise, it is possible to delay the onset of fatigue. But there is no evience supporting any additional benefit from potassium supplements.

The next question becomes: What regulates the potassium levels in the muscle cells? The answer is the nutrient *magnesium, which is amply abundant in most complex carbohydrates. Green vegetables*, because of their chlorophyll content, *are especially rich in magnesium*. Other foods rich in magnesium are nuts, legumes, whole grain cereals and breads, soybeans, and seafood.

A study of trained female cyclists found that as they increased their intake of complex carbohydrates, the length of time they could cycle before they felt fatigued increased. And those cyclists who ate the *most* carbohydrates experienced the most increased "time to fatigue."

Importance of Vitamin/Mineral Intake

Another area to consider in children's exercise is the child's total vitamin/mineral intake. In a careful study of athletes who trained five days a week, for one to two hours a day, it was found that most were getting inadequate levels of B vitamins—particularly vitamin B_1, and minerals such as magnesium and iron. The B vitamins are essential for the conversion of calories to body energy. For this reason, they're an important component in the Eating For A's Program.

Iron is essential for carrying oxygen to oxygen-starved muscle cells. Without that oxygen, all the potassium and magnesium in the world won't do much good. Like many of our children's diets, the diets of the athletes surveyed were found to be more than sufficient in calories but inadequate in the vitamins and minerals needed to convert those calories into energy.

An excellent source of vitamins and minerals for child athletes are Eating For A's Energy Bars (see recipe on p. 234). Although there are many preformulated energy bars in the supermarkets and health food stores, consider the fact that just four Fig Newtons (made without sugar, naturally) will supply at least 200 calories containing 40 grams of carbohydrates, a food packed with energy. Better still, make up a batch of Energy Bars (see recipes at the end of the chapter).

Fat and Exercise

As a parent, the most important thing to realize about your child is that once he reaches adulthood, there is no way to decrease the number of fat cells by exercise or restrictive diets. Some years ago, Rockefeller University conducted an experiment with rats fed barely enough to keep them alive. After about one month, the rats had used up almost all their reserve fat deposits for energy. Soon their bodies began to "eat" their own organs, connective tissue, and muscles. However, *neither the animals' brain cells nor fat cells were consumed*. Fat cells are fully protected during starvation just like brain cells. They grow smaller in size but not smaller in number, like sponges that shrink and swell depending on the amount of water in them. This explains why people gain back so much weight so quickly after being on a calorie-restrictive diet. The weight loss they experience is not due to any loss of fat cells but rather to the cells' decrease in size.

No one is sure whether the number of fat cells in a child is genetically determined or the result of acquired family eating habits. However, both heredity and gender are influential in determining *where* your child's fat cells are likely to accumulate. In females, this tends to be the hips, buttocks, and thighs; in males, it is the abdominal area.

In terms of exercise, an interesting point about fat is that as the intensity of your child's exercise increases, his reliance on fat decreases. This is because fat, in the form of fatty acids, cannot generate or supply enough fuel to the muscles because of the high requirement for oxygen needed in fat metabolism. Carbohydrates, in comparison, require less oxygen and are used more readily by the body during intense workouts.

The worst kind of fat is saturated fat which is linked to coronary disease. Saturated fat triggers the body to produce cholesterol and decreases its ability to excrete and break down excessive cholesterol. Fast-food restaurants are a major source of saturated fats in our diet.

Protein and Exercise

Protein is required to build, maintain, and repair tissue. Unfortunately, a common misconception is that it also supplies immediate energy. For this reason, many athletes consume far more protein than they need each day. Like carbohydrates, protein yields four calories per gram, so it is not fattening. However, unlike carbohydrates, the body must expend a considerable amount of energy to transform protein *into* energy. Protein, therefore, is not a sufficient source of fuel. It only contributes between 1 and 2 percent of the total energy required during exercise.

After your child consumes animal or vegetable protein in his diet, it is broken down in the digestive tract into amino acids and short amino acids called peptides. The body uses these "building blocks" of protein to keep the immune system strong and build new tissue, as well as for many other life-sustaining functions. The body is able to produce some, but not all, of the amino acids it needs. Those that it cannot produce are known as "essential amino acids."

ALTERNATIVES TO RED MEAT PROTEIN

Most parents know that a two-ounce serving of cooked beef is a good source of essential amino acids. However, there are many alternative protein sources which are equivalent to this food. The same number of amino acids could be found in:

3 ounces of crab meat
8 ounces of sardines
2 ounces of canned salmon
2 ounces of chicken, turkey, or duck

2 eggs
5 ounces of tofu
3 tablespoons of dried or canned soybeans
2 ounces of fish
2 ounces of canned tuna fish

Studies have shown that only one-third of the protein in your child's diet needs to come from animal sources. More is not necessary. It is possible to use much less animal protein if you know how to combine incomplete protein foods with one another. (See Chapter 6, Week Four for information on complementary proteins.)

We offer these alternatives because many parents grew up thinking that red meat is a superior source of nutrition for children. The amount of animal fat in the diet increased considerably in the 1950s, reflecting a richer society and a "meat and potatoes" generation with an increased demand for cattle that were fatter. As was the case with the evidence concerning the hazards of cigarette smoking, it took many years of research to discover that there might be health risks associated with red meat.

Today even many athletes are foregoing the pregame steak in favor of foods high in complex carbohydrates. They contend that their endurance increases as their meat intake declines. Separate studies at both Stanford and Harvard University have shown that when it comes to fat, both the amount the body accumulates and excess weight are not linked to how much food you eat each day, or even how many calories you consume—but solely to the amount of fat consumed. Most red meat and animal products are too rich in fat, and for this reason do not fit into any diet directed toward good nutrition and physical fitness.

Ergogenic Aids

Ordinary fitness enthusiasts and highly trained competitive athletes are constantly looking for magical substances to boost their energy and stamina. These supplements are called ergogenic aids. Most of the marketable ones are worthless; a few are even dangerous. For professional athletes, there are *specifically formulated supplements* which are beneficial to their performance, but these products are designed for the particular athlete and the event. A world-class bicyclist in the Tour de France, for example, will burn up over 7,000 calories per day. A recreational bicyclist burns nowhere near that amount, and so cannot benefit from the same level of supplementation.

THE MYTHS OF ERGOGENIC AIDS

Electrolyte replacements: Sports drinks like Gatorade claim to be electrolyte replacements. Children in particular lose very few electrolytes during exercise. After their workout, they are actually in what's called *electrolyte overload* because their bodies have lost more water than electrolytes. These electrolytes can easily be replaced by food, such as the meals in the Eating For A's Program.

Soft drinks: Apart from the problem of carbonation discussed in Chapter 9, soft drinks present other problems. In hot weather, the large amount of refined sugar in carbonated beverages—9 teaspoons per can—delays the time it takes to empty the fluids from the stomach. For some children, the blood sent to the stomach to digest this sugar lowers the blood volume in other parts of the body, raising the possibility of cramps and heat-related illness.

Bee pollen: There's no scientific evidence that bee pollen improves athletic performance in children or adults.

Carbohydrate drinks: Scientists have studied various carbohydrate drinks, including such complex concoctions as glucose polymer solutions. The trouble with such drinks is that although they are fortified with many vitamins and minerals, along with ample calories, they are still short on essential nutrients, such as iron or folic acid, and are relatively expensive. Further, such drinks discourage children from learning how to eat properly to reach peak performance. In the long run, such drinks can be a deterrent to overall good health and long-term athletic performance.

SOME BENEFICIAL ERGOGENIC AIDS

Vitamins and minerals: The foods recommended in the Eating for A's Program provide sufficient levels of vitamins and minerals for peak sports performance.

Water: When children are active and perspire, the drink that they need most is water. It not only regulates your child's body temperature but also cools his active muscles, which prevents soreness. If your child loses too much body fluid through perspiration, there is always the risk of dehydration. A child's body contains between 15 and 25 quarts of water (about 40 for adults), depending on weight, but the loss of even 1 percent after an hour of exercise can seriously affect performance levels.

Fruit juices: Fruit juices, preferably diluted, are another excellent beverage for replenishing minerals and lost carbohydrates, provided they are consumed *following exercise.*

Chromium picolinate: The newest advance for teenagers who are interested in muscular development is chromium picolinate. Discovered by the U.S. Department of Agriculture in the 1970s, it allegedly increases the efficiency of the body's fat metabolism, which means that it helps to burn off fat and increases muscle mass. Unlike body-damaging steroids, it has no dangerous side effects. It also enhances the function of insulin and lowers cholesterol. As of July 1989, numerous NBA players were using it and reporting excellent results. At the moment, there is no research claiming that it benefits youngsters in the Eating For A's age range of 5 to 13 years.

Benefits of Sunlight and Sleep

It is not commonly known that sleep and ultraviolet light work together. The ultraviolet light we receive from the sun releases enzymes in our bodies that can only work in darkness. Sunlight converts some of the cholesterol in the skin to Vitamin D. Therefore, moderate amounts of sunlight are recommended.

In the home or at school, children can benefit from *full spectrum fluorescent lights* that emit low levels of mid- and long-range ultraviolet light. However, it is essential that the diffuser panel, or plastic cover, be ultraviolet transmitting (uvt), otherwise the ultraviolet cannot reach the child's skin.

Studies of elementary school children in both northern Alberta Province, Canada, and Leningrad, U.S.S.R., have shown that such supplementary lights reduce the incidence of absences due to illness and improve academic performance.

What is essential to any child in training is that he receive a certain amount of sunlight during the day. There are, of course, exceptions to this rule. Some athletic children live in climates where daily sunlight is not a common occurrence. But in general, the necessity for sunlight seems to hold true for psychological as well as physical reasons. Depression, tension, and anxiety have all been reported to decrease in children who exercise regularly with the benefit of sunlight.

ENERGY BARS

The following recipe for Energy Bars can easily be prepared in your kitchen. Ingredients may be purchased at your local health food store. Keep the Energy Mix used in making these bars on hand so you can prepare the bars when you need them.

Energy Mix
YIELD: 3 POUNDS

> ½ *pound rice polish*
> ½ *pound wheat germ*
> ½ *pound soy flour*
> ½ *pound dry skim milk*
> ¼ *pound bone meal*
> ¼ *pound brewer's yeast*
> ¼ *pound dulse (kelp powder)*

Combine ingredients and mix well in a large bowl. Place in a tightly capped jar to store.

To Make Energy Bars

> 1 *cup peanut butter (nonhydrogenated)*
> ½ *teaspoon liquid lecithin (may be omitted)*
> ½ *cup peanut oil or soy oil (omit if lecithin is not used)*
> 1 *cup carob powder*
> 1 *teaspoon vanilla extract*
> 1 *cup Energy Mix (approx.)*

Blend the first three ingredients in a mixing bowl. When well mixed, slowly add the carob powder and vanilla. Add enough of the Energy Mix to make a fudgelike consistency. Then press onto a cookie sheet or platter. Add chopped nuts or sunflower seeds if desired. Cut into squares, cool, and store in the refrigerator.

HIGH-ENERGY BREAKFAST IN A GLASS
SERVES: 1
This powerhouse drink can be made the night before and eaten with raw fruit in the morning.

> *1½ cups milk*
> *2 tablespoons nonfat dry milk or soy milk powder*
> *1 tablespoon soy or peanut oil*
> *2 or 3 egg yolks**
> *1 tablespoon honey or molasses*
> *1 teaspoon vanilla extract*

Combine all ingredients in a jar with a tight lid and shake well, or blend in a blender. A banana or other fruit may be added if desired.

---

*Save whites in a jar and refrigerate to use in cooking.

11

EATING FOR A'S
QUESTIONS AND
ANSWERS

These questions are representative of those most frequently asked of the authors. They are broken down into three categories: Parenting, School Lunch, and General Nutrition.

Parenting

Question: My daughter doesn't like to eat brown rice. What suggestions do you have?

Answer: Color counts with children in everything, including foods. Bright colors—red, green, yellow—are fun. So is white. When it comes to rice, most kids would rather eat it white or colored than brown. Actually, brown rice (which is a healthy must) is hardly brown, especially if you wash it properly (see p. 138 for instructions). But you can disguise it by cooking it in chicken broth or tomato juice instead of water. You can make it yellow by adding a pinch of turmeric or saffron to the cooking water; yellow is very appealing. In the beginning, you can make half and half—half brown and half white rice, served Spanish style, with a tomato sauce. Other suggestions on how to be "sneaky" can be found in Chapter 5.

Question: What do I do if my child is allergic to milk? It's everywhere and it's supposed to be essential for children.

Answer: These allergies are often referred to as "lactose intolerance" and are far more common than parents realize. However, there is an increase in available dairy alternatives or milk products specifically manufactured for lactose-intolerant individuals. In addition, the recipes found on pp. 100–193 make it easy for you to make substitutions for milk. The nutrients in milk and other dairy products—namely calcium and protein—can be derived satisfactorily from other foods. Your biggest challenge, of course, is milk chocolate and ice cream, which most children love and which are heavily advertised. Again, there are substitutes such as carob (for chocolate) and nondairy frozen deserts. (Lactose is discussed on p. 48.)

Question: I know sodas interfere with my son's meals. He's 10 years old and when I take him out, he only wants pizza and Coke; then he drinks all the soda and eats half the slice. Also, whenever he plays baseball with his friends, the game always concludes with everyone drinking a soda. It's a social eating habit, and I can't find a way to break it.

Answer: Soda consumption is a hard habit to break, but it can happen over time. If he's interested in sports (as your question indicates) you can point out the disadvantages of soda in athletic competition (see Chapters 9 and 10).

The battle against commercial sodas is one that you'll wage for a while. And it's important that you set guidelines now. To begin with, you can make sure that no soda he drinks contains caffeine; it can be more habit-forming in sodas than in coffee. In fact, there has never been a generation of children whose bloodstreams were so bubbling with carbonated caffeine and energy-draining white sugar. If he keeps it up, your son will be craving a soda in the morning to get him started— just like adults do with coffee.

Once he is drinking caffeine-free soda, you can start reducing the amount he can have during the week, at the same time stocking your refrigerator with the new "healthful" sodas on the market.

Finally you can begin to make your own healthier sodas by simply combining carbonated water with fruit juices (see p. 105). It is best to try these out on your partner and friends first, however. Some favorable comments under your belt will help in dealing with your son's potential critique: "It's yucky!"

Question: My child is not eating properly. He just doesn't seem to have an appetite.

Answer: Most children go through periods when eating seems to be the least of their interests. If you are introducing new foods and he refuses to eat them, or says he isn't hungry, it is best to drop the subject after 15 minutes and simply take the food away. The important thing for the child to realize is that he will not be able to eat again until his regular eating time. Do not offer more until then, so the child does not get the impression he can control you by refusing food.

The most important thing is to avoid conflict over food. It's well known that digestive juices stop secreting and muscles stop contracting when one is faced with stress. One's attitude toward food is created during childhood and is later carried over into adult life.

Question: What does it mean if a child would rather drink than eat? My 7-year-old girl prefers drinking to eating—and not only sodas—milk and juices too. She just doesn't want to sit down and eat.

Answer: Sometimes it's just that the child has a poor appetite and fluids are a lot easier to deal with than solid food. But it can become a vicious circle because if a child gets filled up with fluids he *can't* eat very much. This can lead to nutrient insufficiencies which in themselves may be compounding the problem. It is most important, though, to have the child seen by a doctor since diabetes, kidney disease, and other illnesses are possible explanations for such high fluid intakes.

Question: Is it good or bad for children to drink in the middle of eating their meals?

Answer: You can let your child drink moderately during a meal if he wants to. Some people feel that drinking with meals makes digestion more difficult, but there are no set rules.

Question: Some parents make children anxious about eating. They may say, "You're overweight—don't eat so much;" or "Eat up all the food on the plate—people are starving." How does this affect their digestion?

Answer: The more you make an issue of the child's weight, the more he will resort to eating food if he's overweight, or avoiding it if he's skinny. It is best not to harangue the child; instead, set a good example by eating properly yourself and exercising.

Question: Should children watch television while they're eating? I heard it's not good, but I don't know why.

Answer: We are definitely against children watching television while they're eating, except for special occasions. (See pp. 50 and 60 for reasons.)

Question: How important is it for a child to have a good role model in order to eat healthfully? Can't he be a healthy eater even if his parents aren't?

Answer: Role modeling by parents is one of the major factors in creating healthful eating patterns. See p. 56 for discussion of this.

Question: Should my child be encouraged to finish all the food on his plate, especially if he's eating too little?

Answer: No, only if it's a constant problem. Children's appetites change over the years. Making too much of an issue of undereating has the same implied psychological threats as commenting on overeating. There is some evidence that if a child has no appetite, his zinc levels might be low. A simple test with Zinc Status (Metagenics, San Clemente, California 92672) can determine if a zinc deficiency is at fault. (Directions are on the label.) It is also important to determine if your child has something bothering him; one of the signs of depression in children is loss of appetite. If you suspect something serious, consult the school counselor or a licensed professional therapist.

Question: Should children be allowed to do strenuous exercise right before or after eating?

Answer: A child can do strenuous exercise right before eating. Although most individuals do not have a big appetite immediately after exercising, they will soon after—so be prepared with healthful snacks or meals. It is not a good idea to exercise immediately after eating because the body's blood supply is concentrated in the gastrointestinal tract. Exercise will force the blood supply to feed muscles, disrupting digestion.

Question: When is the best time for my children to do their homework—after school or after dinner?

Answer: Homework should be done when your children can concentrate on it best. Some children like to do their homework while snacking.

Question: My three children have different eating habits—what do I do? Two like greens, one doesn't. One likes soup, the other two don't. What's the solution?

Answer: Get them to agree to support the others' dietary preferences. Fairness should be the doctrine. Serving a favorite soup (e.g., Ninja Turtle soup) five days a week to satisfy one sibling is not fair.

Question: Kids use eating or not eating to get back at their parents. In those instances, when I suspect that my child is acting out, how do I know if it's a genuine lack of interest in the food, or a parental payback?

Answer: You won't unless you ask. A family with an open forum for venting intrafamilial problems won't have to resort to such manipulations.

Question: We don't have much time to talk to our children—but when we try at the dinner table, there are always fights. I know it's not healthy to eat that way, but how do I change it?

Answer: Develop rules of conduct, similar to those preconference rules agreed upon between rival nations. Adhere to these rules; failure to do so or not applying them fairly means that fights will resume. Consider placing a child in charge of monitoring the rules; it might make him appreciate the frustration you experience as a parent in expecting compliance to reasonable rules.

Question: I suspect my daughter is throwing up after eating. I've confronted her, but she denies it. Some of her friends have told me about her behavior. How do I handle it?

Answer: Bulimia (inducing vomiting after eating) is at least 10 times more common in females than males. The bulimic is very ashamed of being out of control and does not want help. Refer the child or adolescent to an eating disorder specialist who can conduct some tests and an interview to determine if your suspicions are warranted. Eating disorder specialists are very familiar with the bulimic's deceptive practices and methods and are empathetic to how difficult it is to stop such behavior.

Question: My child is overweight, yet she doesn't appear to overeat. She's 8. Her doctor isn't taking it seriously. What can I do?

Answer: There is still a feeling that "baby fat" is all right and is something a child will outgrow. Some obesity is controlled by genetic factors, but for the vast majority of children who are significantly overweight for their age, gender, height, and bone structure, obvious consideration should be given to what *kind of food* they're eating (is it too high in calories?), and to their activity level. See discussion of exercise on pp. 213–23 and obesity on pp. 49–52.

Question: There's been a lot of fighting at the dinner table between my husband and my 8-year-old son. My son now wants to eat in his room. How is that kind of tension going to affect his ability to derive nutrition from what he's eating?

Answer: There is growing evidence that intense stress during meals interferes with digestion and absorption of nutrients. If the stress is perceived as intense enough, the child loses his appetite. Wishing to withdraw to the seclusion of his room may just be an adaptive way to eat and won't hinder the food's nutritional benefits. However, if the family finds it impossible to eat with an 8-year-old without severe conflicts, professional assistance should be sought for the whole family.

Techiques that allow everyone to enjoy their meals without conflict can be taught and learned.

Question: My children resent being part of the preparation of food, setting up the table, and cleaning up. How do I show them the importance of that responsibility in regard to food?

Answer: Unfortunately, such responsibilities don't seem really important until the child grows up. Getting a child to accept such chores as a contribution to the family is difficult. This attitude of resentfulness or unwillingness tends to be most common in families where inequitable distribution of responsibilities exists. This includes a father who shirks any responsibilities for setting up the table or cleaning up afterward—the "woman's work" argument. Does your husband (or wife) help with such chores? Children learn avoidance, domination, irresponsibility, etc., from their parents.

School Lunches

Question: The lunches in my child's school are terrible. I don't know how to change them.

Answer: If you have reasons for having your child eat the school lunch, you will want it to be in as much harmony with the Eating For A's Program as possible. And it can be. But you must be prepared to get involved—to become a "change agent." At this point, you are probably saying, "This is ridiculous. What difference can *I* make?" Believe it or not, you *can* make a difference. And that difference will affect the entire school population. You may recall that we spoke about the innovations that the New York City school lunch program adopted in the 1980s. Much of the impetus for this came about through the efforts of parents and other children's nutrition advocates. There is a precedent for change in New York City and other school districts throughout the country and you can build on this. Here, in brief, are some guidelines for improving the school lunch program in your child's school.

1. *Organize:* There's power in numbers, particularly when parents are involved. Get together with other parents who have similar concerns and form a group. It doesn't have to be a large group—just a committed one. If possible, enlist the help of someone within the system. It could be a teacher or school nurse; you don't have to go to the top, just identify someone who shares your views about the food program.

2. *Familiarize yourself with government rules and standards:* If the school participates in the National School Lunch Program, or if it purchases USDA-donated commodities, there are certain standards it must adhere to. There is continual pressure to raise the nutritional standards of lunch in public and private schools, and there are advocacy organizations to give you guidance (see p. 266 for names). With this baseline information, you can be knowledgeable in determining what can be done to improve school meals.

3. *Assess the program:* Analyze menus, ingredients in food, specification standards, and the attitudes and knowledge of those in charge of the food.

4. Establish a policy: Set realistic minimum goals for change and a time frame. Start a nutrition committee composed of parents, students, and teachers plus the food service manager and an administrator. This is an opportunity for everyone to be involved in decision making. There is a precedent for this in many school districts, and it really helps in bringing about results. Here are some important initial changes.

Choices: If your school does not offer choices of lunch items, this should be your first priority. In the beginning, this may simply consist of bowls with salad ingredients (which you can grandiosely call a "salad bar") and a choice of peanut butter or tuna sandwiches (preferably on whole wheat bread) instead of the regular lunch. When children have choices, there is less waste (which pleases the administration); they feel more involved and therefore enjoy lunch more. Choices, therefore, are a small change that has a large impact.

5. *Identify allies in "high places":* There is probably someone in a position of influence who also believes in the need for change. If you publicize your effort, you will probably find that person.

6. *Don't get discouraged:* Just as the changes in your child's diet had to be gradual, so will this. For one thing, you are dealing with a bureaucracy; for another, any change will be met with resistance. But, if you have success in making small changes, you will have a foundation to build on for larger ones. Once change is in the air, there is a momentum that makes the goals easier to achieve.

7. *Change in administration:* The programs in both Helix High School and New York City (see Chapter 1) suffered serious setbacks when their respective administrators left. Both Gina Larson and Elizabeth Cagan were committed pioneers, ready to buck the system for the welfare of the students. It is important to be aware that something unfortunate can happen when a new administrator takes over. This does not always happen, but in any bureaucracy, there is the danger that progress will not be maintained. When a new administration comes in, there is a better chance if advocates lobby for a continuation of policy that is in accord with nutritional upgrading and the changes it takes to insure it.

Having said all this, we want to reiterate that you will probably still have to take the major responsibility for your child's lunch and, at the very least, make sure that you have supplied him with the food to keep him on the program.

Nutrition

Question: What are "cold-pressed" oils, and why are they "better"?

Answer: Cold-pressed oils are considered more healthful because they are less likely to have the chemical residues found in more commercially prepared oils. *Cold pressed* refers to the fact that the oil has been processed at low, rather than high temperatures, and so is less likely to be partially hydrogenated.

Question: Is it really true that vitamin C can cure a child's cold? If so, how much should I give him?

Answer: No, vitamin C cannot *cure* a cold. However, a certain amount of vitamin C each day (between 100 and 500 mg. depending on the child's age), either in food or supplements, can help prevent colds and infections.

Question: I've heard that too much of certain vitamins in food are bad for a child. What vitamins are these? How do I know how much to give?

Answer: Food will never cause a vitamin overdose in a child. Any adverse effects, such as the slightly orange skin color change that comes from eating too much betacarotene in carrots, for example, is transient, nontoxic, and is completely reversible once the amount of that food is cut down.

Question: I've heard that infants would naturally choose the correct foods to eat if a group of foods was placed before them. Why isn't this also true for 5- to 13-year-olds?

Answer: By the time a child is 5, he has formed opinions based on the family and the world about desirable and "yuck" foods. An infant, by comparison, is still relying on instincts.

Question: If a child really hates green vegetables, is it necessary to disguise them? And how seriously should we take those food aversions—can't kids get the same nutrients elsewhere?

Answer: It's really necessary to disguise them if the child won't eat them any other way. (See Chapter 4 for techniques.) Research tells us that the greater the diversity of foods the child eats, the greater the variety he will choose later in life. And variety is what is needed to insure that we get all the required nutrients. For instance, the nutrient folic acid is found in adequate amounts only in a few foods. So, yes, it is important to introduce him to as many vegetables and choices as possible at an early age.

Question: Is it necessary to test a child for a vitamin deficiency when there is a learning disability or an eating disorder such as anorexia?

Answer: Yes, it is necessary. Zinc seems to be a nutrient whose lack is associated with learning disabilities, and also has been shown to play a role in at least 60 percent of patients with eating disorders. A well-trained health practitioner familiar with nutritional tests should be consulted.

Question: When children are hyperactive, what comes first—their hyperactivity or their excessive intake of certain foods?

Answer: It is suspected that hyperactive children develop their vulnerability to certain foods early in life, possibly even *in utero*. To date, no one is certain.

Question: When my children were going to school, I tried to give them healthful foods, but the foods looked so different from what their peers were eating that they refused them. What can I do?

Answer: If your child is old enough, you can help him learn the advantages of the food he eats and why it's special. The most important point is to be creative so that the foods either look like what his friends are eating or are so attractive that his friends will wish they had them! For tips on bag lunches, see pp. 200–03.

Question: In what order should my children eat food: fruit or salad before or after the main course?
Answer: Some lay nutritional writers and alternative nutritionists suggest that certain food groups, such as salads and fruits, be eaten according to some order or time of day. There is no scientific proof that the order in which foods are eaten or the time of day has any nutritional effect.

Question: My husband and I work—is it okay to feed my children food that I've frozen from meals I prepared during the weekend?
Answer: Many foods lose their vitamin value through exposure to air, light, heat, changes in pH (acid/alkaline balance), and age. Freezing retards this loss, with few exceptions.

In regard to generally preserving the nutrient value of foods, fat-soluble vitamins (A, E, D, and K) are more stable than water-soluble vitamins (B vitamins and vitamin C) at high temperatures but deteriorate more upon exposure to oxygen. For this reason, as a general rule, cooking methods should incorporate techniques that use the least amount of heat for the shortest period of time.

The more you cut up a food, prior to heating, the more oxygen can interact with the food to lower its eventual vitamin levels. Even the trace mineral (i.e., iron, copper) content of a food can dictate how much oxygen will lower vitamin levels. This is one reason that some food manufacturers add sodium pyrophosphate, which retards the action of copper, to dehydrated mashed potatoes, thereby reducing vitamin C loss.

Question: How long can food be kept in the refrigerator without losing nutrient value?

Answer: Virtually everyone in North America has a refrigerator. This is part of the reason our supermarkets have such an abundant supply and diversity of foods available at all times. Refrigeration both retards the rate of decay and helps retain nutrient levels in foods. As we've said, heat, light, air, changes in pH, and age affect vitamin levels in food. Most fresh vegetables and fruit should be eaten within 3 to 4 days; meat and fish as soon as possible. Processed foods in containers have expiration dates. Even if the food has been refrigerated, throw it out if it's past the date.

For longer storage of frozen foods, keep them in airtight plastic pouches in the freezer compartment until ready to reheat or cook. This method significantly retards aging, reduces changes in pH, while eliminating exposure to heat, light, and air.

Question: My child seems to have an allergy to the usual proteins: meats, cheese, chicken. What do I substitute? And will he be getting enough nutrients?

Answer: See discussion of complementary proteins on pp. 133–35.

Question: I have a "finicky" eater and don't want to shove food down his mouth. What are the minimum daily nutrients he must receive?

Answer: First, concern yourself with what food your child *likes* to eat. Which of the foods are on the Eating For A's Nutrient List? Of the foods he likes, what vitamins and minerals do they contain? In what quantities? This book gives you the information on wholesome foods and healthy snacks, and with a little homework you'll be able to set up an enriching Eating For A's meal plan.

In addition, have you introduced him to a variety of other foods? "Finicky eaters," as well as some other children, go through developmental stages where they want to have control of their environment. Offering them a limited variety allows children to exercise choice. But these choices should be from the Eating For A's recommended foods.

Question: My daughter had her period at 13 and was regular for one year. She became a vegetarian and has had only one period for the past year. She refuses to eat animal protein. What can I do?

Answer: False menarche is not uncommon. Some girls are so involved with athletics and exercise that they reduce the levels of hormones that promote menstruation. However, amenorrhea is very common in girls with anorexia nervosa. Is she refusing to eat food and consequently underweight? Being a "vegetarian" might be a pretense for avoiding eating. If she is serious about being a vegetarian, it might help to learn something about it yourself, so that you can understand your daughter's position. Then determine if she understands the combinations of foods required for her developing mind and body.

Question: My daughter has a violent reaction to certain foods, and the foods she's allergic to are constantly changing. What about antacids like Tums for children?

Answer: I assume that the reaction you're referring to is behavioral, not allergic. If this is the case, she needs professional assistance. There are clinical psychologists and allergists who specialize in treating individuals with behavioral disorders induced by allergies. Tums and other drugs should not be given to your child until a professional has time to fully evaluate the extent of your child's reactivity. There may even be an emotional trigger that initiates the reactions, another excellent reason to consult a clinical psychologist.

Question: I've heard that "carbohydrate loading" really helps athletes. My children are on the school track team and say they want to "load." What is "carbohydrate loading" and how will it help them?

Answer: In recent years, endurance athletes have talked about loading up on abnormal amounts of glucose to be stored in the muscles as glycogen. This process usually begins six days prior to the date of the competition. The athlete actually depletes glycogen stores in the muscles during these days by eating as little carbohydrate as possible while exercising vigorously. Then for three days the athlete eats as much carbohydrate as possible while exercising minimally.

This process is considered by many experts in sports physiology as a shock to the system and is not generally recommended without proper guidance. Further, for a child who does not run very long distances, the effort of trying to maintain the diet is hardly worth the reward. Regular training under the supervision of a knowledgeable coach would be of far greater value.

Question: I know that candy bars are bad for my children, but it gives them a sort of "pick-me-up" feeling which sometimes keeps them mentally alert. Aren't there some scientists who take a similar position on sodas?

Answer: You should not be confused by any scientists who claim that soda—or any sugar-rich snack—is beneficial to children's mental activity. The studies that they may cite examine only short-term results, without concern for long-term dietary patterns. The answer to a child's lack of alertness is not to give the child a quick energy boost, but to insure that such slow periods disappear completely by feeding the brain in a steady, reliable, and constant fashion.

Question: What are the best kinds of fat for children to eat?

Answer: Scientists to date have demonstrated in animals and humans that the best fats we can include in our diet are those rich in Omega-3 and Omega-6 polyunsaturates. Two common sources of the Omega-3 oils are fish oils, rich in substances called eicosapentaenoic acid (EPA), and vegetable oils made from flaxseed and canola, and some bean and nut oils. These Omega-3 oils are rich in a fatty acid called alpha-linolenic acid. Because vegetarians avoid most sources of saturated fats, they tend to eat relatively more of the Omega-3 fats than meat eaters do. Monosaturated fats, such as olive oil, have also been shown to be healthy for humans.

NUTRIENT VALUES LIST
(Sources of foods richest in each learning nutrient)

You can use this list as a guide when planning menus to supplement the recipes in this book. Only foods high in learning nutrients are listed here; those marked with an asterisk (*) are especially high.

Vitamin A

Dairy Products: Dry nonfat milk powder
Fruit: Mango*, cantaloupe*, papaya*, yellow passion fruit juice*, apricots* and other dried fruits*
Fish: Mackerel (canned), fresh tuna
Meat: Liver (all sources*)—highest content of all foods
Vegetables: Carrots (fresh, cooked, juice*), Swiss chard (cooked*), collard greens (cooked from frozen*), dandelion greens (cooked*), peppers (hot, red chili—fresh, canned), pumpkin (canned*), spinach (cooked from fresh, frozen*), squash (butternut, hubbard—baked*), sweet potato (baked, steamed*), tomato paste (1 cup is almost 3 times higher than 1 cup of tomato sauce; but it will be difficult to use that quantity because tomato paste is so rich, that it will need to be diluted.)
Miscellaneous: Cod liver oil*

Beta-Carotene

The primary sources of vitamin A are fish and animal livers and other animal products (egg yolk, milk, cream, etc.). However, individuals such as vegetarians who prefer not to use animal sources of vitamin A are fortunate in that the precursor of vitamin A, beta-carotene, is readily available in green, yellow, orange, and red plant foods.

253

Thiamin (Vitamin B₁)

Dairy: Kefir drink
Grains: Buckwheat flour (dark), Maypo cereal, oatmeal and rolled oats, semolina (enriched*), whole wheat, wheat germ*, pizza (thick crust), soy milk
Nuts, Seeds: Mixed nuts, peanuts (raw), pistachios (raw*), sunflower seeds (raw), sesame seeds
Vegetables, Legumes: Soybeans, soybean sprouts, squash (acorn—baked provides most of nutrient), tomato paste (See note for vitamin A.)
Miscellaneous: Brewer's yeast

Riboflavin (Vitamin B₂)

Dairy Products: Cottage cheese (low fat), ricotta (part skim), kefir drink, dry nonfat milk powder*, dry buttermilk*, yogurt, plain (low-fat, nonfat)
Grains/Grain Products: Carob flour, oatmeal with bran and raisins, cornmeal (de-germed, enriched), quinoa, soy flour, semolina*, wheat germ (toasted*)
Fish: Clams (canned), mackerel (canned), salmon (canned)
Meat: Liver (calves, veal*)
Nuts, Seeds: Mixed, pumpkin seeds (kernels)
Vegetables: Soybeans (cooked from dry), spinach (cooked from fresh), tomato paste (See note for vitamin A.)

Niacin (Vitamin B₃)

Grains/Grain Products: Oatmeal with bran and raisin, semolina*, corn flour (masa harina*), quinoa pasta, rice bran*, rye (dark), whole wheat
Fish: Salmon, pink, sockeye (canned*), seatrout (Steelhead), swordfish, tuna (canned*)
Meat: Kidney, liver*, chicken (roasted), chicken breast*
Legumes: Tempeh
Nuts, Seeds: peanuts (roasted*)

Vitamin B₆ (Pyridoxine)

Fruit: Avocado (Florida avoados have almost twice the amount as California), banana
Grain/Grain Products: Brown rice, whole wheat bread, wheat germ
Fish: Seatrout, smelts*, tuna, light (water-packed), beef liver*, veal liver
Nuts, Seeds: Sesame seeds (dry*), soybeans (dry, roasted*), sunflower seeds (dry, roasted*), walnuts
Vegetables, Legumes: Garbanzos (canned*)
Miscellaneous: Garlic powder*, brewer's yeast

Folic Acid (Folacin)

Vegetables/Legumes: Spinach (fresh*), kale, watercress, parsley, asparagus, broccoli, mushrooms, soybeans
Grains/grain products: Wheat germ (toasted*), soy flour*
Nuts, Seeds: Pumpkin seeds*, sesame seeds*, sunflower seeds
Meat: Turkey (liver*)
Other: Egg yolk, brewer's yeast
Note: The folacin of egg yolk, liver, and brewer's yeast is better absorbed than that from other sources.

Anywhere from 45 to 95 percent of folic acid may be destroyed by boiling, prolonged cooking, or exposure of the food to excess heat, as for example in canning. Vegetables stored at room temperature lose up to 70 percent of their folic acid within three days.

Vitamin C (Ascorbic Acid)

Fruit: Black currant juice*, orange juice (fresh*), papaya*, strawberries
Vegetables: Broccoli (cooked from fresh*), sweet red pepper (cooked from fresh), red pepper (raw*), tomato paste (See note for vitamin A.)

Iron

Fruit Juice: Raspberry juice, fresh*

Grains/Grain Products: Amaranth*, cream of wheat cereal, oatmeal, quinoa pasta*, rice bran, rye flour (dark), soy flour (defatted), wheat germ (toasted)

Fish: Clams (canned*), oysters, Eastern and Pacific (raw or simmered)

Meat: Beef heart, liver, chili with beans

Nuts, Seeds: Almonds, cashews (raw*), pistachios (raw*), sesame seed kernels (raw*)

Vegetables/Legumes: Jerusalem artichokes, potato flour*, soybeans (cooked from dry), tomato paste (See note on Vitamin A), tofu (firm*, soft)

Miscellaneous: Blackstrap molasses*

Magnesium

Grains/Grain Products: Amaranth*, buckwheat, whole (dry), buckwheat flour, dark, corn flour, cornmeal (boiled), oat bran, rolled oats, oatmeal, quinoa pasta*, soy flour, whole wheat flour, wheat germ (toasted* and raw)

Fish: Clams (canned*), mackerel (canned), Eastern Oysters, (simmered), pink, sockeye salmon (canned)

Meat: Chili with beans

Nuts, Seeds: Almonds (raw*), Brazil (raw*), cashews (raw or roasted*), filberts (hazelnuts*), Macadamia (raw), peanuts*, sesame seed kernels (raw), soybeans (roasted: Roasted soybeans can be eaten like nuts and are different from dry soybeans, which are cooked as a bean), sunflower seed kernels, walnuts

Vegetables/Legumes: Black beans (cooked), lima beans (cooked from fresh), white beans (cooked from dry), yardlong beans (cooked from dry), Swiss chard (cooked), soybeans (cooked from dry), spinach (cooked), tofu (firm, soft)

Potassium

Dairy Products: Nonfat dry milk powder*, dried buttermilk*, yogurt (low fat, nonfat)

Fruit: Avocado (Florida*—higher; California*), banana, plantain*, raisins (dark*)

Grains/Grain Products: Amaranth*, quinoa pasta*, rice bran*, soyflour (low-fat*, defatted*), wheat germ (raw*, toasted*—higher)

Fish: Clams (drained*), salmon (canned, Atlantic*, pink sockeye*—even higher), snapper (baked, broiled), trout (baked, broiled), tuna (canned in water)

Meat: Chili with beans

Nuts, Seeds: Almonds*, Brazil*, cashews*, mixed nuts*, peanuts*, pistachios (raw*), pumpkin seed kernels (roasted*), soybeans (roasted*), sunflower seeds (raw*)

Miscellaneous: Spaghetti sauce (homemade*)

Vegetables/Legumes: White beans (baked from dry*), lima beans (cooked from fresh*, dry*), navy beans (cooked from dry, canned), pinto beans (cooked from dry*), refried beans (canned*), beet greens (cooked*), Swiss chard (cooked from fresh*), lentils (cooked from dry*), potatoes (baked*), potato flour*, soybeans (cooked from dry*), acorn squash (baked*), Hubbard squash (baked*), tomato paste (See note on vitamin A), tomato puree*, chili sauce (tomato based*), tempeh*

Miscellaneous: Blackstrap molasses*

Zinc

Dairy Products: Ricotta cheese (part skim), dry nonfat milk powder

Grains/Grain Products: Amaranth*, whole wheat flour, wheat germ (raw*, toasted*)

Fish: Clams (canned*), Alaska King crab leg*, blue crab*, lobster*, mackerel (canned), Eastern oyster* (All oysters are high; Eastern have the highest content of all foods), Pacific oyster*, salmon (canned, pink sockeye)

Meat: Chuck (lean*), round tip (lean*), veal cutlet (lean*), rib*, heart*, turkey (dark meat*)

Nuts, seeds: Almonds*, cashews*, filberts (hazelnuts*), peanuts, pecans, pumpkin/squash seed kernels (whole), walnuts, sesame seed kernels (raw*)

Miscellaneous: Miso (soybean paste*)

Chromium

Dairy Products: Yellow cheese*

Wheat, Wheat Products: Whole wheat bread, wheat cereal, tortilla chips (taco flavor)

Fruit: Prunes*, apple juice*

Nuts, Seeds: Peanuts (raw*), peanut butter* (higher than peanuts)

Fish: Oysters

Foods Containing Multiple "Learning Nutrients"

Chilies, raw	Vitamins A, C, niacin
Chilies, dried	Vitamins A, niacin, iron
Dried mixed fruit	Vitamin A, potassium, iron
Brewer's yeast	Zinc, niacin, vitamins B_1, B_2
Avocado, Florida	Iron, niacin, vitamins B_1, B_6
Tuna	Zinc, niacin, potassium, vitamin B_6
Banana	Potassium, vitamin B_6
Wheat germ	Zinc, magnesium, folic acid, vitamin B_1
Chicken giblets	Iron, zinc
Skim milk, dry	Magnesium, vitamin B_1, vitamin B_2, vitamin A, potassium
Dried apricots	Vitamin A, potassium
Canteloupe	Potassium, vitamins A, C
Sardines	Potassium, iron
Salmon	Niacin, potassium, folic acid

REFERENCES

American Heart Association. *1987 Heart Facts*. American Heart Association: Dallas, TX, 1987.

Barrett, D. E., Frank, D. A. *The Effects of Undernutrition on Children's Behavior*. Gordon and Breach: New York, 1987.

Baynes, R. D., Bothwell, T. H. Iron deficiency. *Annual Reviews of Nutrition*, 1990: 10; 133–148.

Beaton, G. H. Variability of nutrient requirements in the human. In: Velázquez, A. Bourges, H. [Eds.] *Genetic Factors in Nutrition*. Academic Press: New York, 1984.

Bernat, I. Iron deficiency. In: *Iron Metabolism*. Plenum Press: New York, 1983, pp. 215–274.

Bjoerntorp, P., Vahouny, G. V., Kritchevsky, D. [Eds.] *Dietary Fiber and Obesity*. Alan R. Liss: New York, 1985.

Bouchard, C., Shephard, R. J., Stephens, T., Sutton, J. R., MacPherson [Eds.] *Exercise, Fitness and Health: A Consensus of Current Knowledge*. Human Kinetics: Champaign, IL, 1989.

Brewster, L., Jacobson, M. F. *The Changing American Diet*. Center for Science in the Public Interest: Washington, D.C., 1982.

Bryce-Smith, D. Environmental chemical influences on behavior, personality, and mentation. *International Journal of Biosocial Research*, 1986: 8; 115–150.

Campbell, S. B. *Behavior Problems in Preschool Children: Clinical and Developmental Issues*. Guilford Press: New York, 1990.

Chandra, R. K. [Ed.] *Trace Elements in Nutrition of Children*. Raven Press: New York, 1985.

Committee on Atherosclerosis and Hypertension in Childhood of the Council of Cardiovascular Disease in the Young and the Nutrition Committee, American Heart Association. AHA position statement: Diagnosis and treatment of primary hyperlipidemia in childhood. *Arteriosclerosis*, 1986: 6; 685A–692A.

Conners, C. K. *Food Additives and Hyperactive Children*. Plenum Press: New York, 1980.

Consensus Development Conference. Lowering blood cholesterol to prevent heart disease. *Journal of the American Medical Association*, 1985: 253: 2080–2086.

261

Dakshinamurti, K. B vitamins and nervous system function. In: Wurtman, R. J., Wurtman, J. J. [Eds.] *Nutrition and the Brain, Volume 1*. Raven Press: New York, 1977.

Dawber, T. R. *The Framingham Study: The Epidemiology of Coronary Heart Disease*. Harvard University Press: Cambridge, MA, 1980.

Delight, S. Special foods help lower injuries for Helix high school athletes. *San Diego Union*, April 1, 1962.

Dhopeshwarkar, G. A. *Nutrition and Brain Development*. Plenum Press: New York, 1983.

Dobbing, J. [Ed.] *Early Nutrition and Later Achievement*. Academic Press: New York, 1987.

Dodge, P. R., Prensky, A. L., Feigin, R. D. *Nutrition and the Developing Nervous System*. C. V. Mosby: St. Louis, 1975.

Egger, J. Food allergy and the central nervous system. In: Reinhardt, D., Schmidt, E. [Eds.] *Food Allergy*. Raven Press: New York, 1988.

Franklin, A. J. [Ed.] *The Recognition and Management of Food Allergy in Children*. Parthenon Publishing: New York, 1988.

Galler, J. R. The behavioral consequences of malnutrition in early life. In: Galler, J. R. *Nutrition and Behavior*. Plenum Press: New York, 1984.

Galli, C., Simopoulos, A. P. [Eds.] *Dietary ω3 and ω6 Fatty Acids. Biological Effects and Nutritional Essentiality*. Plenum Press: New York, 1989.

Gaulin, S. J. C., Konner, M. On the natural diet of primates, including humans. In: Wurtman, R. J., Wurtman, J. J. [Eds.] *Nutrition and the Brain, Volume 1*. Raven Press: New York, 1977.

Gifft, H. H. Washbon, M. B., Harrison, G. G. *Nutrition, Behavior, and Change*. Prentice-Hall: Englewood Cliffs, N.J., 1972.

Gracey, M., Falkner, F. [Eds.] *Nutritional Needs and Assessment of Normal Growth*. Raven Press: New York, 1985.

Hersen, M., Eisler, R. M., Miller, P. M. [Eds.] *Progress in Behavior Modification*. Academic Press: New York, 1983.

Horrobin, D. F. Essential fatty acids, psychiatric disorders, and neuropathies. In: Horrobin, D. F. [Ed.] *Omega-6 Essential Fatty Acids*. Alan R. Liss: New York, 1990.

Leibel, R. L., Greenfield, D. B. and Pollitt, E. Iron deficiency, behavior, and brain chemistry. In: *Nutrition Pre- and Postnatal Development*. Winick, M. [Ed.] Plenum Press: New York, 1979, pp. 383–439.

Lessof, M. H. [Ed.] *Clinical Reactions to Food*. John Wiley & Sons: New York, 1983.

Lester, M. L., Thatcher, R. W., Monroe-Lord, L. Refined carbohydrate intake, hair cadmium levels, and cognitive functioning in children. *Nutrition and Behavior*, 1982: 1; 3–13.

Lonsdale, D. A *Nutritionist's Guide to the Clinical Use of Vitamin B-1*. Life Sciences Press: Tacoma, WA, 1987.

Lonsdale, D. Shamberger, R. Red cell transketolase as an indicator of nutritional deficiency. *American Journal of Clinical Nutrition*, 1980: 33; 205–211.

Lyman, B. *A Psychology of Food, More Than A Matter of Taste*. Van Nostrand Reinhold: New York, 1989.

Miller, S. A. [Ed.] *Nutrition and Behavior*. Franklin Institute Press: Philadelphia, 1981.

Nutrient Adequacy: Assessment Using Food Consumption Surveys. National Research Council. National Academy Press: Washington, D.C., 1986.

O'Banion, D. R. *An Ecological and Environmental Approach to Behavioral Medicine*. Charles C. Thomas: Springfield, IL, 1981.

Olson, R. E. Safety and vitamin and mineral supplements for mother and child. In: Berger, H. [Ed.] *Vitamins and Minerals in Pregnancy and Lactation*. Raven Press: New York, 1988.

Pollitt, E., Leibel, R. L. [Eds.] *Iron Deficiency: Brain Biochemistry and Behavior*. Raven Press: New York, 1982.

Pollitt, E., Metallinos-Katsaras, E. Iron deficiency and behavior: constructs, methods, and validity of the findings. In: Wurtman, R. J., Wurtman, J. J. [Eds.] *Nutrition and the Brain, Volume 8*. Raven Press: New York, 1990.

Pollitt, E. *et al*. Behavioral effects of iron deficiency anemia in children. In: *Iron Deficiency, Brain Biochemistry and Behavior*. Pollitt, E. and Leibel, R. L. [Eds.] Raven Press: New York, 1982, pp. 195–204.

Prinz, R. J., Roberts, W. A., Hantman, E. Dietary correlates of hyperactive behavior in children. *Journal of Consulting and Clinical Psychology*, 1980: 48; 760–769.

Rapp, D. J. *The Impossible Child*. Practical Allergy Research Foundation: Buffalo, N.Y., 1989.

Recommended Dietary Allowances, 10th Edition. National Research Council. National Academy Press: Washington, D.C., 1989.

Rindi, A., Patrini, C., Cominsiolo, V. Brain vulnerability to thiamine depletion. *Brain Research*, 1980: 181; 369–380.

Rumsey, J. M., Rapoport, J. L. Assessing behavioral and cognitive effects of diet in pediatric populations. In: Wurtman, R. J., Wurtman, J. J. [Eds.] *Nutrition and the Brain, Volume 6*. Raven Press: New York, 1983.

Schauss, A. G. Effects of environmental and nutritional factors on potential and actual batterers. In: Roy, M. [Ed.] *The Abusive Partner: An Analysis of Domestic Battering*. VanNostrand Reinhold: New York, 1982.

Schauss, A. G. Evidence of zinc deficiency in anorexia nervosa and bulimia. In: Essman, W. B. [Ed.] *Nutrients and Brain Function*. Karger: Basil, 1987.

Schauss, A. G. Nutrition, academic achievement and behaviour disorders: Applying the research to schools. *Health at Schools* (U.K.), 1988: 3; 182–186.

Schauss, A. G. Nutrition and behavior. *Journal of Applied Nutrition*, 1983: 35; 30–43.

Schauss, A. G. Nutrition and behavior: Complex interdisciplinary research. *Nutrition and Health* (AB Academic), 1984: 3, 9–27.

Schauss, A. G. Nutrition and social behavior. In: Bland, J. *1984–85 Yearbook of Nutrition Medicine*. Keats Publishing: New Canaan, CT, 1985.

Schauss, A. G. The effects of nutrition on brain function, behavior, and learning: Directions for integrative research. *International Journal of Neurology*, 1989: 23; 111–115.

Schoenthaler, S. J., Doraz, W. E., Wakefield, J. A. Jr. The impact of a low food additive and sucrose diet on academic performance in 803 New York City public schools. *International Journal of Biosocial Research*, 1986: 8; 185–195.

Schoenthaler, S. J., Doraz, W. E., Wakefield, J. A. Jr. The testing of various hypotheses as explanations for the gains in national standardized academic test scores in the 1978–1983 New York City nutrition policy modification project. *International Journal of Biosocial Research*, 1986: 8; 196–203.

Serban, G. [Ed.] *Nutrition and Mental Function*. Plenum Press: New York, 1975.

Shneour, E. *The Malnourished Mind*. Doubleday: New York, 1974.

Shoemaker, W. J., Bloom, F. E. Effect of undernutrition on brain morphology. In: Wurtman, R. J., Wurtman, J. J. [Eds.] *Nutrition and the Brain, Volume 2*. Raven Press: New York, 1977.

Sobal, J., Muncie, H. L. Vitamin/mineral supplement use among adolescents. *Journal of Nutrition Education*, 1988: 20; 314–318.

Somogyi, J. C., Hötzel, D. [Eds.] *Nutrition and Neurobiology*. Karger: Basil, 1986.

Spring, B. Effects of foods and nutrients on the behavior of normal individuals. In: Wurtman, R. J., Wurtman, J. J. [Eds.] *Nutrition and the Brain, Volume 7*. Raven Press: New York, 1986.

Stekel, A. [Ed.] *Iron Nutrition in Infancy and Childhood*. Raven Press: New York, 1984.

Strong, J. P. Coronary atherosclerosis in soldiers: A clue to the natural history of atherosclerosis in the young. *Journal of the American Medical Association*, 1986: 256; 2863–2866.

Tucker, D. M., Sandstead, H. H., Penland, J. G., Dawson, S. L., Milne, D. B. Iron status and brain function: Serum ferritin levels associated with asymmetries of cortical electrophysiology and cognitive performance. *American Journal of Clinical Nutrition*, 1984: 39; 105–113.

Turner, M. [Ed.] *Nutrition and Lifestyles*. Applied Sciences Publishers: London, 1980.

Webb, T. E., Oski, F. A. Behavioral status of young adolescents with iron deficiency anemia. *Journal of Special Education*, 1974: 8; 153–156.

White, P. L., Selvey, N. [Eds.] *Malnutrition: Determinants and Consequences*. Alan R. Liss: New York, 1984.

Willet, W. C., Stampfer, M. J., Colditz, G. A., Rosner, B. A., Speizer, F. E. Relation of meat, fat, and fiber intake to the risk of colon cancer in a prospective study among women. *New England Journal of Medicine*, 1990: 323; 1664–1672.

Winick, M. *Malnutrition and Brain Development*. Oxford University Press: London, 1976.

Wohlfarth, H. and Hargreaves, J. A. The effect of middle and long wave ultraviolet radiation from full spectrum lighting on the incidence of absences due to illness in school-aged children. *International Journal of Biosocial and Medical Research*, 1990: 12; 130–132.

Zamkova, M. A. and Krivitskaya, E. R. The effect of middle and long wave ultraviolet erythema lamps on visual reception and performance of school-aged children. *International Journal of Biosocial and Medical Research*, 1990: 12; 125–129.

Worthington-Roberts, B. Suboptimal nutrition and behavior in children. In: *Contemporary Developments in Nutrition*. C. V. Mosby: St. Louis, 1981, pp. 524–562.

SUGGESTED READING

American Wholefoods Cuisine, Nikki & David Goldbeck, New American Library: New York, 1983.

Confessions of a Sneaky Organic Cook, Jan Kinderlehrer, Rodale Press: Emmaus, PA, 1971.

Consumer Beware, Beatrice Trum Hunter, Simon & Schuster: New York, reprint Bantam, 1972.

Earth Water Fire Air: A Cookbook for the 90s, Barbara Friedlander Meyer, Philosophical Library, 1990.

The Fast-Food Guide, Michael Jacobson & Sarah Fritschner, Workman Publishing Co.: New York, 1986.

Feed Your Kids Right, Lendon Smith, M.D., Dell Publishing Co.: New York, Delta, 1979.

Sugar Blues, William Dufty, Warner Books, New York, 1975.

The Tassajara Bread Book, Edward Espe Brown, Shambala Publications: Berkeley, CA, 1970.

CHILD NUTRITION ADVOCACY ORGANIZATIONS

American Nutritionists' Association
15200 Shady Grove Road, Suite 350
Rockville, MD 20850

Center for Science in the Public Interest (CSPI)
1501 16th Street, N.W.
Washington, D.C. 20036

Institute for Child Behavior Research
4182 Adams Avenue
San Diego, CA 92116

Feingold Associations of the United States
P.O. Box 6550
Alexandria, VA 22306

Food Research and Action Center (FRAC)
2011 Eye Street N.W.
Washington, D.C. 20006

Physicians Committee for Responsible Medicine
P.O. Box 6322
Washington, D.C. 20015

Public Voice for Food & Health
1001 Connecticut Avenue, Suite 522
Washington, D.C. 20036

INDEX

Abstract thinking, 1
Academic performance, 1, 9, 12–13, 14, 19, 51
Acting out, 18
Advertising, 63
    television, 9–10
Aesthetics (food), 86
Agar-agar, 122
Allergies, 35, 40–49, 249, 250–51
    exercise and, 220
    milk, 46, 48–49, 237
    relief from, 49
Alpha-linolenic acid, 252
Amasake, 122
Amenorrhea, 250
American Academy of Pediatrics, 215, 216
American Cancer Society, 212
American Institute of Biosocial Research (AIBR), 7
American Journal of Cardiology, 218
American Medical Association, 14
American Nutrition Society, 12
Amino acids, 133, 134, 229
Anemia, 30
Animal protein, 133, 229–30
Anorexia nervosa, 52, 53–54, 250
Antacids, 250–51
Anxiety, 234
Appetite, 238, 239, 240
Appetizers, 109, 126, 135–36, 149, 166
Arrowroot, 122
Artificial colors/flavorings, 11, 33, 35, 36, 39, 41, 70, 79
    allergies to, 46
    avoiding, 109
Athlete's Mix, 95–97

Athletic performance, 1, 12–13, 14, 19
    sports nutrition and, 224
    see also Exercise
Attention span, 25, 31, 39
Attitude
    exercise and, 219, 222–23

B vitamins, 227
Bag lunches, 86, 200–03
    hot foods in, 201–02
Bannister, Roger, 210–11
Beans, 162–63
Bee pollen, 232
Behavior, 5–6, 9, 19, 39, 61
    sugar and, 47
Behavior change, 18, 35, 43
Behavior problems, 27
    allergies and, 46
    iron deficiency in, 30–31
Behavioral contracting, 57–59
Beta-Carotene, 253
Bettelheim, Bruno, 55
BHA, 37, 38, 79
BHT, 37, 38, 79
Binge eating, 52
Bioavailability, 34
Birthday parties, 206–07
Blood sugar level, 38–39
Bogalusa Heart Study, 199–200
Bone density, 220
Boston University, 13
Brain
    chemical equilibrium of, 24, 25–26
    diet and, 18–19, 24–25
    effect of food additives on, 36–37
Brain function, 6–7, 18–19, 104
    iron in, 30